THINK TANK LIBRARY

CAVEAT!

By 1998, neuroscientists could use positron emission tomography (PET) to observe and measure the elasticity of the developing brain, along with the rate of what is technically called synaptogenesis!

In plain English, this means that scientists are now able to measure brain development. In fact, they have evidence showing that children ages 4 to 10 generate new brain synapses at a rate double that of adults, and developing brains keep up the growth pace past teenage years.

This should be a warning to teachers and librarians in no uncertain terms: Carpe diem! Now is the time when opportunity knocks! *Students are ready to think, hard-wire new knowledge, and understand their world.*

Chugani, Harry. "A Critical Period of Brain Development: Studies of Cerebral Glucose Utilization with PET." *Preventive Medicine* 7 (1998): 184–188. (And many other scientists subsequently.)

THINK TANK LIBRARY

BRAIN-BASED LEARNING PLANS FOR NEW STANDARDS, GRADES 6–12

Mary Boyd Ratzer and Paige Jaeger

AN IMPRINT OF ABC-CLIO, LLC
Santa Barbara, California • Denver, Colorado • Oxford, England

Library of Congress Cataloging-in-Publication Data

Ratzer, Mary Boyd.
   Think tank library : brain-based learning plans for new standards, grades 6-12 / Mary Boyd Ratzer and Paige Jaeger.
      pages cm
   Includes bibliographical references and index.
      ISBN 978–1–61069–988–4 (paperback) — ISBN 978–1–61069–989–1 (ebook) 1. School libraries—United States. 2. School librarian participation in curriculum planning—United States. 3. Inquiry-based learning—United States. 4. Education—Standards—United States. 5. Middle school libraries—Activity programs—United States. 6. High school libraries—Activity programs—United States. 7. Thought and thinking—Study and teaching (Middle school)—United States. 8. Thought and thinking—Study and teaching (Secondary)—United States. I. Jaeger, Paige. II. Title.
   Z675.S3R26   2015
   027.80973—dc23   2014032126

ISBN: 978–1–61069–988–4
EISBN: 978–1–61069–989–1

19 18 17 16 15   1 2 3 4 5

This book is also available on the World Wide Web as an eBook.
Visit www.abc-clio.com for details.

Libraries Unlimited
An Imprint of ABC-CLIO, LLC

ABC-CLIO, LLC
130 Cremona Drive, P.O. Box 1911
Santa Barbara, California 93116-1911

This book is printed on acid-free paper ∞

Manufactured in the United States of America

CONTENTS

ACKNOWLEDGMENTS

The following teacher-librarians contributed lesson ideas or lesson pilot feedback for this book. This field testing and field contribution adds to the strength of the content. It showcases the co-operative resource-sharing characteristic for which our profession is known.

Aimee Bishop, Social Studies Teacher, Brittonkill High School, New York

David Brown, Social Studies Teacher, Saratoga Springs High School, New York

Amy Carpenter , School Librarian, Stillwater Middle High School, New York

Steve Danna, PhD, Dean of Branch Campus, SUNY Plattsburgh at Queensbury—colleague and local brain research advocate

Michele Furlong, School Librarian, Brittonkill High School, New York

Jason Groark, Social Studies teacher, Salem High School, Salem, New York

Tim Jacques, ELA Teacher, Brittonkill Hgh School, New York

Wendy Jacques, ELA teacher, Shenedehowa High School, Clifton Park, New York

Kathy Mayba, Social Studies Teacher, Shenedehowa High School, Clifton Park, New York

Jan Tunison, Scotia Glenville High School, Scotia, New York

INTRODUCTION

WHY THINKING? THINK TANKS, PROBLEMS, AND CREATIVITY— A BEAUTIFUL MIND

A crisis arose in our household years ago, when a March thaw, combined with heavy rain, flooded our basement. As buoyant objects began to float about and water rose to above the ankles, a panic beset the dad of the house, as he locked in on rising water with no apparent way to stop it or get rid of it. Evacuation and selling the wrecked house for peanuts were the best ideas he could come up with.

Enter six-year-old David, deflecting parental frenzy.

Attempting to initiate a quiet in the storm, a time to think and consider, he stated: "Now wait a minute. Just let me think. I will figure something out. I am a problem solver."

Indeed, in grade 1, his teacher had framed her year with problem solving and transparent thinking. Her thinkers internalized the skills. Later, *Dave the Thinker* invented a number of innovative devices to solve family problems, such as a dog foot washer to prevent dirty dog tracks on the kitchen floor.

Floods notwithstanding, David represents his species. He is, as we all are, a problem solver. Equipped with a short-term memory that has a finite capacity, our complex brains are wired to solve problems as a key to survival. We can access and process data, employ it to set learning goals, and create solutions. Our brains consolidate and diffuse bits and pieces into meaningful concepts. They predict with a discipline specific knowledge base, categorized to quickly fit circumstances that arise.

Inquiry learning and project-based learning are powerful essentially because they are brain based. Some correlations between inquiry and brain-based learning include:

- Building of background knowledge, big ideas, and vocabulary of the discipline
- Tapping of prior knowledge and prior attitude
- Building strong real-world scenarios
- Making personal choices
- Investigating experientially
- Using multiple resources in many formats
- Coaching and feedback at point of need
- Making emotional connections
- Interacting socially
- Constructing meaning

- Focusing on connections
- Ongoing questioning
- Reflecting on metacognition
- Seeking and evaluating information
- Forging patterns, relationships, and building big ideas
- Wondering and curiosity that engages the learner

Recent decades have given birth to cognitive science, introducing educators to how the brain works. Applying brain science to learning allows us to improve teaching and student performance. Many books have been written about *brain science* and this book does not intend to compete with that vast body of research. However, that same research has led us to the positions we espouse in this book as applied to our work of educating students.

Inquiry is the framework for the deep, brain-based learning experiences in this book. Fostering deep thinking and the development of an *expert mind* is the central focus of this book. The assumption that classrooms and schools can be think tanks will be demonstrated in the sample lessons. Truly, if they are not think tanks, classrooms will diminish their potential to implement the Common Core Learning Standards. They diminish their potential to move beyond rote, and fact-soaked brains with no possibility for content mastery.

The progression of the novice brain to the expert brain is the heart of the matter for college and career readiness. Progression from novice to expert brain is our responsibility and our charge. It is essential to achievement and our economic future. We are educating the next generation that will run the world. This mission is not only critical, it is imperative.

Universities have the impression that K–12 educators require only rote and recall from their students. This advice to professors from Columbia University is incriminating:

Students must recognize the limitations of their current skills, knowledge, and perspectives. They must realize that approaches rewarded in high school—such as rote memorization, the mechanical use of formulas, or the parroting back ideas from a textbook—are no longer sufficient in college, where we value originality, high-level analytical skills, and facility in writing.
http://www.columbia.edu/cu/tat/pdfs/Transformational%20Teaching.pdf

This book is an amalgamation of brain research. Our bibliography represents years of reading, learning, embracing, and implementing brain-based educational recommendations. We did not do the research, but we assimilated this and put it into practice. It is time to take thinking seriously and equip the leaders of tomorrow to change our world!

CHAPTER I

THINK TANKS AND THE CULTURE OF SCHOOL

The pure, original think-tank phenomenon inspired this book. Although the prototype is not a perfect match for the culture of a school, the Common Core does encourage a culture of collaboration true to the think-tank model. Think tanks are essentially defined by expertise, collaboration, research, and focus on a *problem.* This can easily be mirrored in a library, classroom, or a school.

Pinterest is populated with think-tank classroom ideas. Prepackaged think-tank bulletin board die cuts, student awards, and stickers are for sale on Google. Also, many project-based and inquiry-driven classrooms feature think-tank spaces, think-tank resources, and instructional goals related to thinking.

A virtual tour of think-tank culture in schools abounds in colorful manipulatives, activities, and brain teasers. A think-tank tour would include student-directed investigations, collaborative learning ventures, real-world experiences, and problem solving. Think-tank references align into three tiers:

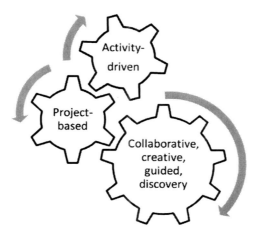

Tier three genuinely encompasses the best thinking, as well as collaborative, creative, and problem-centered student work. This requires a supportive learning environment in which students are safe to question, investigate, brainstorm, and refine their discoveries based upon information, evidence, and thought. At this level, knowledge of the discipline and its language is the starting point.

Think tanks are real world. Generating and advocating for public policy is often done in a think-tank model. Government and corporate interests support think tanks to address problems, issues, and

Does this foster College and Career Readiness	Does this work for a think-tank model?	Objectives aligned with the Common Core and College and Career Readiness:
✓	✓	Research to deepen understanding
✓	✓	Communication of original and unique ideas
✓	✓	Speaking and listening in a climate of critical engagement
✓	✓	Synthesizing data and texts
✓	✓	Shaping useful habits of mind, thinking dispositions, and thinking skills
✓	✓	Connecting to problems and issues in the real world

opportunities. Scientific research often occurs in a think-tank setting. NASA solved the problems with *Apollo 13* in a frenzied, collaborative, and problem-based crisis, and the mission was saved by expert thinking. The economy and the well-being of millions are pushed forward daily by think tanks in informal, low-profile settings.

Some aspects of the Common Core dispose classrooms and teachers to use a think-tank approach to problems and issues. Using knowledge for a meaningful purpose requires higher level thought. Primary source texts, background knowledge, and key concepts generate topics to be explored, uncovered, and investigated.

Think-tank classrooms and think-tank schools transform learning with purpose, energy, and motivation. Learners can experience genuine flow in their collaborative work, moving beyond the clock and irrelevant tasking. Learners can enjoy awareness of cognition and successful solutions. New ideas, pride in rigorous work, and purposeful analysis reward those in think-tank classrooms and think-tank schools.

CHAPTER 2

TWENTY-TWO BRAIN-BASED STRATEGIES TO MAKE YOUR LIBRARY A *THINK TANK* TODAY

Consider the following suggestions as brain basics. You can optimize instruction and learning by using these brain strategies in your library or classroom. If you weave these in routinely, there will be a significant difference in the dynamics of your library. A learner-centered environment generates and stimulates thinking. Using these multipurpose *think-tank tools* often results in innovative ideas to take thinking to a new level. Conscious use of these tools can become habitual and natural. Skill increases with use. Each strategy aligns with research on how the brain learns and what works optimally for active learners.

It is the supreme art of the teacher to awaken joy in creative expression and knowledge.

Albert Einstein

1. **Elicit emotion**
   When emotion is in play, the brain focuses better and remembers what is learned. Carefully pay attention to emotion, a much underestimated component of learning. Motivation, purpose, and personal connections all thrive when emotion is tapped. Emotion can transform a disaffected learner and generate enthusiasm in a student who does not care. Music, film, stories, pictures, and experience help trigger an emotional response.

2. **Connect, connect, connect**
   Short-term memory has a finite capacity. The brain can move many facts into long-term memory by chunking details under broad categories. Charting, concept mapping, mind mapping, and Web 2.0 tools visualize connections and help to discern relationships among discrete items. Connecting elements of text to experience, or people to ideas, doubles the likelihood of getting the brain to pay attention and file the idea into memory. Otherwise, it will be treated like background noise. Consciously connect new content to prior knowledge. Recycling ideas, essential questions, and concepts strengthens neural pathways. Conventional wisdom says: *neurons that fire together wire together.*

3. **Talk, socialize, interact, collaborate**
   The human brain is hardwired for social interaction. Learning in a solitary and silent mode is not optimal for memory. Learning in a socially interactive setting is characterized by sharing, feedback, discussion, critical engagement, or conversation. This "turns on the lights" for the brain, as Ross Todd posits. The quality of decisions made with peer involvement surpasses those generated solo.

Knowledge products produced collaboratively by teams that merge diverse talents and strengths are stronger than those created by one mind.

4. **Be quiet**

   After an interval of multitasking or diverse learning experiences, the brain has a tough job to accomplish. To process important new ideas, the brain needs to consolidate what it has in temporary holding. This complex activity requires a quiet, inactive time such as a break, or even sleep. Taking multiple breaks at intervals from sustained activity gives the brain its quiet time to go to work consolidating. Intense, sunrise to sundown exposure to media, relentless entertainment, and minute-to-minute texting defeats the brain's efforts. Sleep is the last resort.

5. **Think aloud**

   Model your expert brain in action, verbalizing what you are thinking. Call attention to the thinking process when solving problems or tackling tough text, when making an important decision, or weighing pros and cons. Place a real or virtual sign over your doorway: Thinking in progress. Activate your brain. This is often referred to as metacognitive modeling.

6. **Challenge with rigor**

   It is counterintuitive, but the brain responds to rigorous content with equally rigorous thinking. Nature seeks the easy path, and brains do too. Quick decisions and a surface grasp of concepts appeal to the line of least resistance in the brain. Many learners think they know when they are merely familiar with a concept. This can be a barrier to really knowing content. Low-level thought is not likely to get neurons firing or connecting. Rigorous and meaningful work actually leads to deep understanding, when the brain grapples with understanding, reasoning, questioning, and evaluating. Dilemmas are valuable and worth a thousand flat, airless facts.

7. **Engage the power of reflection and metacognition**

   Self-assessment, metacognitive thinking, and the habit of evaluating one's own progress all boost learning and the quality of products. Stopping to consider what is accomplished against a model, a rubric, or a reflection with a peer helps the learner to confront problems and use feedback to improve performance. A fast-track task that starts like a footrace, whisks through the essentials, and lands in the done pile with a thud can be completed without thinking. Unfortunately, the thinking makes the learning happen. Thinking is the true essential.

8. **Question**

   Questions are catalysts of thinking. Thinking is the catalyst for learning. Learning is ultimately not based on answers, but on questions. Questions can spark curiosity, probe deeper reasons, clarify foggy notions, or challenge assumptions. Questions redirect the flow of ideas back to the learner. They uproot misconceptions and insist on better evidence. Questions scaffold understanding from what to how and why. Questioning is at the heart of the Common Core because of its connection to thinking.

9. **Answer questions with questions**

   Every librarian has heard his or her share of "stupid questions" despite the old claim that there is no such thing. We beg to differ. We can answer those questions with other questions to help metacognitively model the path of deductive reasoning. When you hear a stupid question such as, "Do you have any good books?" you can respond with the better mode, "Well, how do you define 'good,' Johnny?"

10. **Solve authentic problems**

    The human brain is a problem-solving brain. Failing to use the power of authentic problem solving in teaching and learning is like pushing a high-powered sports car up a hill. So much content easily converts into a problem-based framework. It is like turning on the ignition and roaring down a thinking highway. The beauty of problems is that they have no immediate answers. Brains need to analyze, evaluate, synthesize, and conclude to work with them. That level of thinking assures transfer and long-term new knowledge.

11. **Be relevant**

    What does this have to do with me? When will I use this again in my life? Why should I care? Students and the brain keep asking those questions. In an efficiency-driven and energy-saving screening process, the brain is constantly dismissing and forgetting the irrelevant. Mental survival does not depend on spelling words or practicing fractions. Hooking a concept area to the learner's own life experience is a bridge prescribed by the Common Core State Standards CCSS. If learning is relevant to the real world and to the learner, the brain processes the incoming information with attention.

12. **Synthesize**

    Bloom's Taxonomy and newer iterations of Depth of Knowledge and Cognitive Rigor stack levels of thinking from rote and recall on the low end to synthesis at the high end. The thinking and concluding that discerns connections among the related, and even the unrelated, is synthesis. Synthesis is the catalyst for transfer. Transfer means that a learner will be able to use new knowledge in other applications. Transfer means cognitive real estate is in place where new and related understanding can grow. Stopping short of synthesis reverts learning back to rote and recall of facts.

13. **Deconstruct and reconstruct**

    Breaking down texts, content, and information into structural and conceptual chunks pulls the brain's focus back to usable big ideas and relationships. Analyzing broad or complex data (information or evidence) into sense-making chunks increases the likelihood that the brain can wrap itself around new information or knowledge. Looking for patterns, themes, or universal historical frameworks can facilitate mental footholds. Instead of an overwhelming buzz of tiny info-bits, the brain reconstructs pieces into a reasonable and logical web. Building that cognitive frame or schema results in confidence and stamina that sustain thinking.

14. **Inquire and question**

    The inquiry process is an amazing composite of brain-based strategies. Indeed, each step in the inquiry sequence has a brain-friendly process in place. *Wonder, investigate, synthesize, express* are innately brain-based steps richly connected to higher level thought. Turning to a learner-centered, knowledge-centered, question-driven, collaborative, and interactive learning model is the one-stop shopping option too good to pass up. Engaged learners care, personalize connections, think to solve problems, and address issues. They communicate and reflect. Inquiry-based learning is ideal to launch thinking.

15. **Manipulate, fool around, play**

    Daniel Pink would approve of right-brained strategies to incubate creativity and innovation. Einstein would also agree. Experimentation, hands-on manipulation, experience with robotic software, open-ended engineering dilemmas, and other ways to save the world lend themselves to epiphanies or discoveries or theories. Makerspaces participatory software, hands-on materials, STEM components, and creative manipulatives deserve our attention and space.

16. **Probe the schema**

    Learners arrive at your door with a pre-existing set of notions about almost everything they have encountered in life. Wind happens because trees move. There is no connection between shifts in the distribution of wealth and the decline of labor unions. The way to get more money is to shop and get lots of change. Air quality does not have anything to do with me. The case in point is that librarians can open up a conduit to the schema. The strategies to revisit misconceived ideas and break the robust tethers of wrong thinking are the portals to understanding the world.

17. **Teach thinking skills**

    Go ahead. Direct instruction of thinking skills with guided practice is the straight path to a goal. Learners need to figure out how to think more expertly. Age-appropriate target thinking skills are illustrated in this book. Feedback, stopping to reinforce evidence of thinking, and reflection strengthen the thinking pathways in the brain.

18. **Mix it up, jazz it up!**

Variety is definitely the spice of life, and the spice of thinking. The brain is always saying to itself: "What's different? What's new?" Nietzsche's famous quote, "Even the gods are bored," is probably true enough. Learners grind down to glassy-eyed sloggers when the input is a droning remake of yesterday's course. This is not complicated. Take a visual approach today, an auditory approach tomorrow. Dance, sing, and sculpt the way they do in Waldorf Schools. Get kids to generate captions and cartoons. Make iMovies. Recreate a living historical event on the Underground Railroad. Use the whiteboard today, the Library of Congress photo archive tomorrow. Speak, listen, and read aloud. Interview. Take digital pictures. Write a collaborative poem, a dialog. Virtually visit the poles or the bottom of the sea. Skype. Blog. Publish or take a trip. The possibilities are endless.

19. **Inquire: Use Socratic dialog**

Ultimately, evidence of understanding needs to be elicited. Demonstrate that safe little packaged answers are often going to be poked and expanded. Ask, *What do you mean?* Create a culture of critical engagement. Use Socratic questioning to convince learners that inch deep will not cut it. *Can you say that in another way? Why would you assume that? Have you experienced that yourself? What evidence exists that this is true? Where did you find that information? Is that a reliable source?* Make that skeptical posture a regular part of your repertoire.

20. **Add choices and voices**

The importance of choice and personal voice cannot be overstated. Once again, turning the tables and making the learner the center of the dynamic lights up the brain like a 4th of July picnic. Communicating original conclusions, making decisions, solving problems, and addressing meaningful issues get the gears turning. The learner is invested. Motivation kicks in. Ownership changes everything. Personal agency, according to Ross Todd, is the result of this shift. The learner can say with confidence: "I care. I count. I can."

21. **Ensure safety and reduce stress**

When the brain is stressed, it reverts to a flight-or-fight mode that is not amenable to learning or thinking. Still in touch with survival instincts, the brain is distracted by fear, uncertainty, threats, worry, or suffering. Making the library a safe learning environment is a fundamental and essential predisposition to thinking and learning. Comfort, respect, stimulation, opportunity, community, success, and support can be built in everyday for everyone.

22. **Generate and create, then celebrate!**

Research on writing, reading, and thinking recommends the principle that all learners need to be productive. Publishing, posting, sharing, displaying, and creating would show up in an MRI of the brain like the lights of Times Square. A celebratory moment rejuvenates, bonds, and prompts the all-important reflection. Work that does not matter finds its way into trash cans or into high school lockers for cleanout day. What has been meaningfully accomplished, as a generative and collaborative learner, will brighten the light of the mind indefinitely.

CHAPTER 3

THINK-TANK LIBRARIES AND INQUIRY

When is a question the answer?
When is solving a problem the perfect way to engage learners?
When is rigorous and challenging work the best kind?
When does collaboration and communication super-charge learners?
When is brain-based learning firing and wiring neurons?

The answer is: *When the library is a think tank!*

Learning theory confirmed by neuroscientists has infused the Common Core, the new C3 Framework for Social Studies, and the Next Generation Science Standards. The common thread, which is more like a rope binding these together, is inquiry learning. The rationale for this is straightforward: it works. Learners reach deep and lasting understanding of their world through inquiry.

Can school librarians see themselves in these standards? Are school librarians optimizing the power of brain-based learning? Are they innovating to be ready for critical thinking and information literacy so

evident in these standards? This is a time of incredible opportunity. School librarians need to engage with the C3 Framework and its inquiry-bones: *developing questions, planning inquiries, evaluating sources, using evidence, and communicating conclusions and taking informed action.* School librarians need to celebrate Inquiry in the Next Generation Science standards. They need to engage with their problem-solving approach and the embedded ELA standards that lead to writing, research using multiple sources, arguments, and evidence-based claims.

Our 2014 book *Rx for the Common Core: A Toolkit for Implementing Inquiry Learning* explicitly defines the power of inquiry to engage and empower learners. Real-world guidance for teachers and librarians evolved from over six years of embedded coaching in real schools.

Inquiry has deep roots in brain research. Understanding how kids learn is the basis for effective pedagogy. Many instructional practices ignore brain research and get poor results. Passive learners who listen to learn retain very little of what they hear—perhaps as little as 5 percent after two weeks. Active learners engaged in inquiry achieve long-term understanding of content. Essential questions and big ideas drive deep understanding and the construction of meaning. Learning characterized by background building, attention to prior knowledge, questioning, investigation, original conclusions, synthesis, and communication results in lasting and flexible new knowledge.

One path to growing inquiry is WISE. WISE is an acronym meaning Wonder, Investigate, Synthesize, and Express. The WISE Inquiry Model provides a script for an inquiry-based learning experience. WISE is compact and diligently grounded in successful curricular models. These models begin with an overarching, essential question aimed at the learning objective. This model embraces higher level thinking.

Students have shared their voices in reflection on WISE, the inquiry model they use in pursuing their research investigations:

Essential questions

"Behind all of our amazing work, we have questions to answers and we call them Essential Questions. These questions are very important to us because they tell us what we are going to do our research on. Our most important Essential Questions for the whole year have been, 'Why does where we live change how we live?' and 'Why is it important to learn about the world?' I have learned information about some countries that made me think differently about them."—Middle School Student

Using a mentor text

"By learning about New Zealand first, now I understand what I will be investigating for all of my countries."—5th Grade Student

Wonder

"Wonder is the first step in the W.I.S.E. process for inquiry learning. When we wonder, we are actually beginning our research. We start by thinking of an Essential Question that will help us focus when we research. In our World Scrapbook binder, we have wonder words to help us think. Some of them are how, compare, explain why, and describe." —5th Grade Student

Investigate

"When I investigate, it makes me think. When I have to figure out something on my own, I feel responsible for my work and I'm doing more than just reading. I'm investigating to find answers to my own questions." —11th Grade Student

Synthesize

"The 'S' in W.I.S.E. stands for synthesis. Synthesize means to organize the information we found from our sources. When we are done researching, we take our information and put our notes onto our colored note-taking templates. We put all the information in our own words so that we understand."—Secondary Student

Express

"The 'E' in W.I.S.E. stands for Express. When we express our learning, we show what we have learned in a creative way. Some of the ways we have expressed our learning have been making graphs, Wordles, and art projects. We have also written paragraphs and reported to the others in our UN groups."

—Shared with enthusiasm by school librarians Liz Bailey and Jan Tunison, grade 5 teacher Karen Robbins, her students, and Principal Lisa Mickle, who have taken the inquiry path

A complete copy of the WISE Inquiry model can be found in *Rx for the Common Core: A Toolkit for Implementing Inquiry Learning* by Mary Ratzer and Paige Jaeger, Libraries Unlimited 2014.

CHAPTER 4

THINKING AND THE COMMON CORE

In a broad view, the Common Core is an engine to transform the content and delivery of learning. Tapping research that posits the importance of reading and comprehending complex text, the CCSS acknowledges that critical thinking alone does not improve student performance. However, driving principles of the CCSS align with brain-based learning and the power of thinking. If the CCSS had headlines, they would certainly read:

Higher Standards Focus on Rigor and Relevance
Deep Understanding Linked to Synthesis
Real-World Problem-Solving: Part of Multidisciplinary Approach
Writing Evidence-Based Claims Taps Critical Thinking Skills

Selected evidence from the CCSS solidifies the role of thinking in the standards:

Use their experience and their knowledge of language and logic, as well as culture, to think analytically, address problems creatively, and advocate persuasively.

Delineate a speaker's argument and specific claims, evaluating the soundness of the reasoning and relevance and sufficiency of the evidence and identifying when irrelevant evidence is introduced.

Present claims and findings, emphasizing salient points in a focused, coherent manner with relevant evidence, sound valid reasoning, and well-chosen details.

Propel conversations by posing and responding to questions that probe reasoning and evidence; ensure a hearing for a full range of positions on a topic or issue; clarify, verify, or challenge ideas and conclusions; and promote divergent and creative perspectives.

Respond thoughtfully to diverse perspectives; synthesize comments, claims, and evidence made on all sides of an issue; resolve contradictions when possible; and determine what additional information or research is required to deepen the investigation or complete the task.

Present information, findings, and supporting evidence, conveying a clear and distinct perspective, such that listeners can follow the line of reasoning, alternative or opposing perspectives are addressed, and the organization, development, substance, and style are appropriate to purpose, audience, and a range of formal and informal tasks.

CHAPTER 5

NOVICE AND EXPERT THINKERS

```
WANTED:
Expert Thinkers
```

That sign hangs on the door of college admissions offices, corporate human resources suites, and small-business front doors. College and career readiness inherently demands that young learners succeed in their passage from novice to expert thinkers.

The learner who is a thinker-work-in-progress can be spotted in a school library with a simple task assigned by a health teacher:

Students need to identify and access a single periodical article about the impact of drug use on American teens. A discussion of the articles retrieved would build background knowledge for the class. They would later initiate research on specific problems caused by drug use in high school.

How is this young man a novice thinker? Let us count the ways:

1. Googler skimmed his choices.
2. Googler picked a short and probably unsuitable piece for the purpose at hand.
3. Googler did not read closely. If he did, it might have made him aware that he was probably going to come up short in the survey of information ahead in the classroom.
4. Novice thinker bypasses the problem with the text and reads it without a critical perspective.
5. Novice thinker is glad to be done with the task.

Obviously the student lacks deep knowledge of the content area, and also does not care about the content area enough to engage or exert effort. This information pandemic is rampant in our schools with many classroom teachers joining this misinformation mode-of-operation. With one-to-one device initiatives pervasively showing up in classrooms, it is imperative to understand why this model of fact fetching is rife with problems.

Accessing the Internet instead of a
database, the novice thinker plugs a
broad search statement into Google.

The first few hits are scanned.

The selection of a very brief review of a
book about drugs convinces the student
that his task is complete.

Printing a postage stamp block of text, a
librarian encounters the student and
points out the problems with the book
review as a useful resource.

Glad to have his work done for the period, the
student insists that the article will be fine and
proceeds to finish his math homework.

WHAT IS WRONG WITH SIMPLE FACT FETCHING?

- Isolated details from the book review will do little to construct a meaningful schema
- Facts have a brief shelf life in short-term memory
- Anemic information-fragments, sliced from a website, will not connect to or build concepts or connections
- Whatever prior knowledge or attitude this learner holds will stay in place
- Misconceptions, partial understanding, and wrong ideas live on
- With a fuzzy, partly-constructed mental model of the subject at hand, this learner has no chance to get to the valid and productive questions that will kick start new knowledge
- This learner begins a passage to expertise from a universal base camp of novice actions, judgments, and thinking

Teachers and librarians can be guides for a successful passage to *expert thinking. Conscientiously engaging the novice in these steps makes thinking teachable:*

How does this list of strategies uncover the characteristics of expert thinkers? Research by many, including De Groot, Glaser, Wineberg, Brandsford, Donovan, Pellegrino, Marzano, Cleary, Zimmerman, Ericsson, and Bruer elucidated numerous common elements in expert thinking. Experts seem to have what could be called an *Effective Thinking Model.* Teachers and librarians, especially in collaboration, can motivate and guide learners to internalize facets of expert thinking. This book embeds that process in real-world models. When expert thinking is unified into a model, these key elements are consistently present. Note how combining the elements correlates with synthesis.

Building background knowledge sufficient to construct meaning	Taking time to build understanding by framing the content in *big ideas*	Framing learning in a problem or essential question
Setting goals for learning	Eliciting prior knowledge and attitudes making flawed notions transparent	Engaging the learner in personal connections to the content
Establishing relevance with the learner in an active role	Motivating learners to plan in order to solve a problem	Modeling the relationships between details
Thinking aloud and modeling higher-level thinking (metacognition)	Using higher-level questions to clarify, deepen, and critique	Leading discussion to capture student thinking
Making misconceptions transparent	Interrogating fact, opinion, opposing ideas, and multiple perspectives	Engaging learners in critical analysis
Supporting the learner in connecting discreet bits of information with concepts	Modeling the organizational structure of new knowledge through relationships	Emphasizing patterns in new knowledge and their role in meaning
Using the big ideas to provide a mental model of the content area	Sustaining learners in close reading as a base for questions	Expecting solid evidence

Expert learners are:

Resourceful and knowledgeable	Strategic and goal directed	Purposeful and motivated
• Bring considerable prior knowledge to new learning	• Formulate plans for learning	• Are eager for new learning and are motivated by the mastery of learning itself
• Activate that prior knowledge to identify, organize, prioritize, and assimilate new information	• Devise effective strategies and tactics to optimize learning	• Are goal-directed in their learning
• Recognize the tools and resources that would help them find, structure, and remember new information	• Organize resources and tools to facilitate learning	• Know how to set challenging learning goals for themselves
• Know how to transform new information into meaningful and useable knowledge	• Monitor their progress	• Know how to sustain the effort and resilience that reaching those goals will require
	• Recognize their own strengths and weaknesses as learners	• Monitor and regulate emotional reactions that would be impediments or distractions to their successful learning
	• Abandon plans and strategies that are ineffective	

Used with Permission: National Center on Universal Design for Learning, udlcenter@udlcenter.org

While every lesson will not display all these elements consciously, the goal is to foster expert thinking in your students so that these characteristics are observable in discussion, investigation, brainstorming, and concluding. That accomplished, we should feel successful.

Beginner thinker: Observer, recorder	Novice thinker: Asks questions, wonders why
Follows directions to complete tasks	Seeks answers
Records observations	Transfers facts
Identifies facts	Challenges thinking
Sees no patterns or connections	Understands basics, then asks questions
Records as directed	Transfers meaning—does not create new meaning.
Completes task cooperatively	Big ideas still under construction
Meaning is not constructed	Clusters related facts under a main idea
May develop vocabulary for future use	Relies on short-term recall
Traps the right answer	Does not fully understand

Augmenting thinker: To build upon, to change	Expert thinker: Innovator
Constructs meaning from text	Uses vocabulary of the discipline knowingly
Uses big ideas and conceptual frameworks	Understands relevant concepts deeply
Connects prior knowledge	Understands big ideas
Connects personal relevance	Plans, strategically develops goals
Develops focus questions	Gathers information, answers why
Seeks and uses information	Seeks to understand to solve
Builds arguments with evidence	Uses the known to solve the unknown
Evaluates quality of sources	Creates new meaning
Incorporates multiple perspectives	Pursues quality information
Understands the problem, issue	continually assessing validity, bias, perspective, purpose, opposing ideas, and gaps
Takes and supports a position	
Creates new meaning	Organizes new information by concepts
Draws conclusions	Self-assesses
Synthesizes seemingly unrelated facts into new knowledge	Communicates with a clear point of view
Debates, interrogates, self-assesses	Improves
Communicates reasonably, logically	Challenges positions and justifies

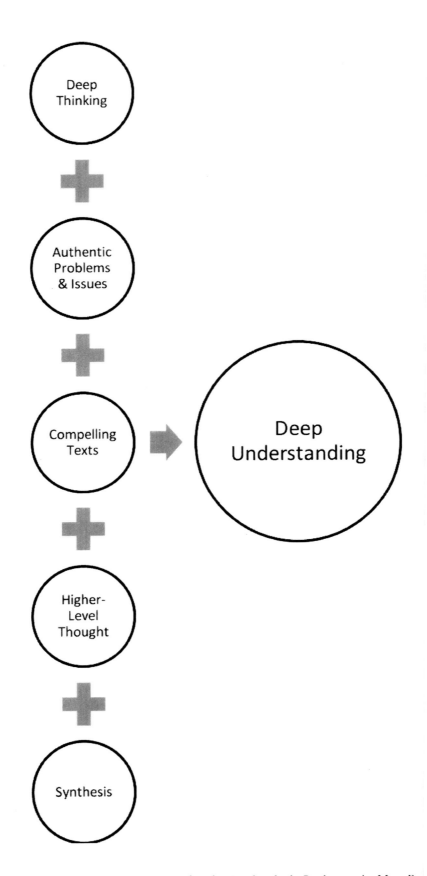

From *Think Tank Library: Brain-Based Learning Plans for New Standards, Grades 6–12* by Mary Boyd Ratzer and Paige Jaeger. Santa Barbara, CA: Libraries Unlimited. Copyright © 2015.

CHAPTER 6

IF THE BRAIN COULD TALK

If a learner's brain could talk to a teacher, what important and strategic points would it try to convey? What reminders would it share? What insights could we gain? The voice of the cognitive scientist would affirm these basics and encourage educators to complete a reality check. Are you optimizing instruction for the brain?

- My short-term memory is limited and does not last very long.
- I am constantly processing a lot of information.
- I am very elastic and making the most synapses from ages 4 to 10.
- I attach new knowledge to old knowledge … somehow making a connection.
- I consolidate patterns so that I can store more related information in chunks. I can classify items into categories to help me store them in the long- term memory.
- The more I already know about something, the easier it is to know more.
- Some input comes from the background around me and some gets more of my attention.
- I tend to monitor and screen out information that is low contrast, because it overloads my circuits.
- I delete things with no value.
- For important information to get my attention it has to have a contrast to the hum of the influx.
- To handle all that information coming in, I have to combine pieces and bits that are related.
- I can quickly filter what is important and not important, once I have experience with information.
- Engage me by spotlighting importance: make it personal, curious, experiential, connected, or real.
- I pay attention to what is unique, emotional, different, or exciting.
- I function exceptionally well with social interaction, and stimulating experiences.
- I use knowledge flexibly and apply it when I understand it better.
- I consolidate facts that are new when I am sleeping or quiet, not when I am playing video games or texting.
- Knowing the vocabulary of new information helps me to learn it.
- Fluency in thinking gets better with knowledge of the subject and its vocabulary.
- I can synthesize and evaluate information.

CHAPTER 7

THINKING AND INFORMATION LITERACY

A WORD GAME

Sort the following actions into two categories: critical thinking and information literacy. If an action fits both categories, place it in both boxes, and reflect on your results.

Analyzing   Synthesizing   Reflecting   Self-assessing   Comparing/contrasting
Categorizing information   Identifying a problem   Solving a problem   Evaluating
Inferring   Discerning connections   Drawing conclusions   Supporting a claim   Conceptualizing
Arguing with evidence   Sorting fact and opinion   Questioning   Assessing evidence
Exploring multiple perspectives   Organizing   Communicating   Interpreting

Thinking	Information Literacy

This exercise might serve as an object lesson. Every action in the text box belongs in the domain of critical thinking as well as in the domain of information literacy. Mutually reinforcing and coexisting, the two occupy the same space at the same time in an active learner's mind. This has many implications.

Surveying the benchmarks of cognitive development and thinking skills, connections to information literacy and problem solving are not only evident but pervasive. One could argue convincingly that expert thinking is the key to competence, confidence, and success in any number of contexts. Inextricably linked in a powerful alliance, thinking and information literacy join forces in the journey from novice to expert thinker. Arguably, cognitive development, thinking, and information literacy are interdependent. They merge, reinforce, and blend in the cognitive growth of the child and adolescent.

When higher order thinking skills are enumerated, problem solving, synthesis, inquiry, and metacognition are always identified. The CCSS challenges learners to use critical thinking when closely reading texts, engaging in discussion, writing evidence-based claims, and supporting arguments. All of these depend on information literacy skills that help construct original conclusions with synthesis.

Transforming rather than transferring information requires thinking. Developing focus questions and investigating begins the process. Constructing meaning from multiple texts involves critical thinking. Big ideas evolve from analytical thought, seeking relationships among discrete or even oppositional ideas. Exploration of possible solutions to authentic problems demands a carefully planned inquiry. Diligent assessment of quality of information, validity of conclusions, and relative importance of evidence requires critical thinking and constitutes information literacy.

Comprehension and fact finding, ascertaining the right answer, or searching for the authority with the correct viewpoint do not add up to higher order thinking. Making the learner responsible for drawing conclusions, setting a goal, or investing in a real-world solution gears up the level of thinking exponentially. It also gears up the likelihood of long-term understanding. A developing intellect constructing big ideas, sorting fact from opinion, supporting arguments with evidence, and self-assessing demonstrates aspects of expert thinking and information literacy skills. In using facts and details to support reasoning, reconciling conflicting or incomplete information, and incorporating multiple perspectives, a young thinker is information literate.

Theorists who have analyzed thinking processes, including Marzano, Harada, Hester, Crowl, and Facione, agree that thinking and information literacy converge when learners:

- identify problems, discern issues, seek solutions,
- set a learning goal; plan and develop questions,
- investigate by evaluating and using information or data,
- verify the reliability, importance, usefulness, and credibility of information or data,
- organize information, synthesize, use evidence to support an argument, communicate,
- self-assess, reflect.

These steps are the information literacy process, and these steps are thinking.

CHAPTER 8

THINKING IN ENGLISH LANGUAGE ARTS

The significant problems we face cannot be solved at the same level of thinking we were at when we created them.

Albert Einstein

A Junior Great Books discussion question for the story of *Jack and the Beanstalk* could set the stage for an overview of thinking in ELA: Did Jack solve his problems in the air or on the ground? The beauty of this question is that it has no apparent or immediate answer. Multiple threads of plot and character need to be woven together to arrive at a conclusion. Analysis and a rudimentary evidence-based claim could be part of the considered response. The brain is engaged in resolving a question with many possible answers.

In one local high school, an interdisciplinary course for grade 10 students merged global history and English. Rigorous expectations regarding a final oral presentation loomed over the motivated and the not-so-motivated students. This oral report started with a work of world literature; each student had their own. Research requirements included the folllowing:

- The literary criticism of the work over time
- The history of the time period in which the work was written
- The history of the time period in which the work was set
- Biographical information about the author

The research stage of this project was steep indeed, and the thinking required of a student put more than one brain in traction. Generating a thesis required convergence of all these areas and some actually found their thesis in critical texts regarding the work. Others authentically synthesized and pursued their own idea.

Often the outcomes were stellar, and energizing to the student who accomplished the work. This illustration might capture the thinking. Reading *The Lark* by Jean Anouilh, mining the history of Nazi-occupied France, where the work was written, and grasping the history of fifteenth-century France, where the work is set, was accomplished. A young thinker concluded that Anouilh's role in the French resistance and the parallel chaos in the times of Joan of Arc came together in this thesis: in times of political collapse and chaos, strong women are needed.

To some degree traditional instruction in ELA deferred to comprehension, vocabulary, plot, characters, theme, chapter tests, five paragraph essays, and the ubiquitous book report. The vignettes offered above are real world, but also date back decades. Deep thinking, analysis, and synthesis have always characterized ELA literacy. Inquiry with its rich repertoire of thinking skills is no stranger to ELA, and NCTE endorses inquiry in its newest framework for curriculum. (See below.)

With the CCSS shifts, thinking in ELA extends to nonfiction texts and literacy in social studies, science, and technical subjects. Universal skills for college and career readiness stem from ELA competencies and thinking in that discipline. Arguments based on evidence, literary evidence-based claims, development of thesis statements, and interrogation of multiple perspectives are all targets set by higher education for graduates of K–12. ELA has shifted to authentic texts, problem solving, and communication using many tools, including the Internet and digital applications.

Scaffolding reading and writing competencies, the CCSS builds learning on questioning, thinking, evaluating, and concluding. The deeper the level of knowledge, the more complex and comprehensive the level of thinking. Collaboration, speaking, and listening extend thinking and critical engagement. The National Council of Teachers of English (NCTE) emphasizes thinking in their *Framework for 21st Century Curriculum and Assessment*. Some of their literacies include the following:

- Manage, analyze, and synthesize multiple streams of simultaneous information.
- Create, critique, analyze, and evaluate multimedia texts.
- Independently and collaboratively solve problems as they arise in their work.
- Build on another's thinking to gain new understanding.
- Use inquiry to ask questions and solve problems.
- Critically analyze a variety of information from a variety of sources.
- Solve real problems and share results with real audiences.
- Make connections between their work and the greater community.
- Create new ideas using knowledge gained.
- Synthesize information from a variety of sources.
- Use information to make decisions.

National Council of Teachers of English. *NCTE Framework for 21st Century Curriculum and Assessment*. Copyright 2013 by the national Council of Teachers of English www.ncte.org. Reprinted with permission. http://www.ncte .org/governance/21stcenturyframework. 19 April 2014.

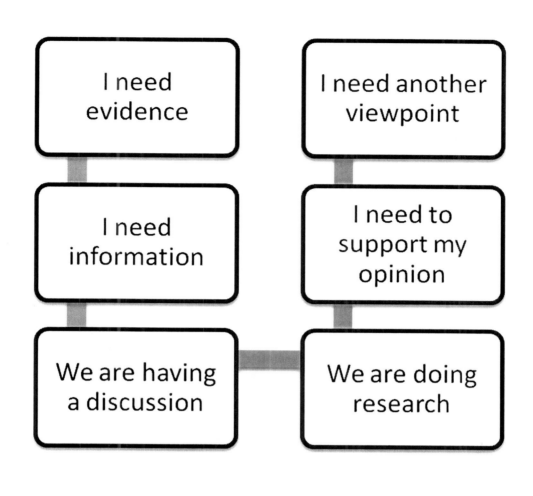

I need evidence	I need another viewpoint
I need information	I need to support my opinion
We are having a discussion	We are doing research

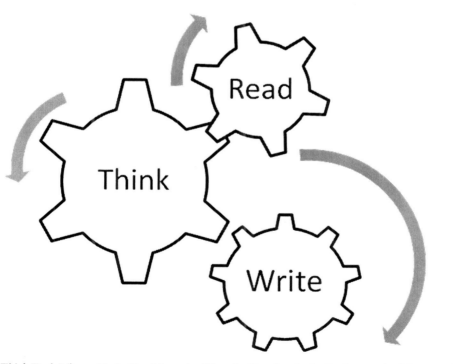

Read

Think

Write

Low level Thinking in ELA	Higher level Thinking in ELA
Remembering	Producing and planning
Recalling, retrieving explicit details	Questioning to inquire, questioning across multiple texts
Giving examples	Deciding about the theme
Categorizing, matching	Focusing on audience and purpose
Restating, paraphrasing	Evaluating for bias, relevance, criteria
Identifying main ideas and supporting details	Using reason and logic
Explaining cause and effect	Validating, verifying and citing with evidence,
Predicting	Developing alternatives, multiple perspectives
Answering who, what, where, when questions	Concluding what the central message is
Making text to self comparisons	Generating, creating new knowledge
Describing	Evaluating claims, organizing, distinguishing relationships
Summarizing	Comparing text to text
Sorting opinion and fact	Analyzing problems, issues or viewpoints
Applying writing conventions	Using syntax and word choice to communicate effectively
Critiquing the text	Synthesizing across multiple texts

CHAPTER 9

THINKING AND TEXT-DEPENDENT QUESTIONS

Common Core pedagogy shifts include close reading for textual details, evidence, and deep meaning. This often happens in English, reading, and the library. However, this generation has an aversion to reading and prefers pictures over print. In order for us to motivate our students to scrutinize and deeply understand the meaning of a primary source document, a book, a passage, an article, or another text, we may have to ask questions that guide their comprehension. These questions are often referred to as text-dependent questions (TDQs).

In our scheduled library time, we can carefully craft our discussions following the recommended pattern below. We start off at the panoramic level asking general and obvious questions—not assuming all students know the basics. From there we can move to concrete fact-type questions which establish the basics of the passage. Once the groundwork has been laid with general and concrete questions, we can move to questions that are challenging. These myopic questions may address a specific CCSS standard such as main idea or inference. From there we can aim for interpretations and deep meaning based upon evidence in the text.

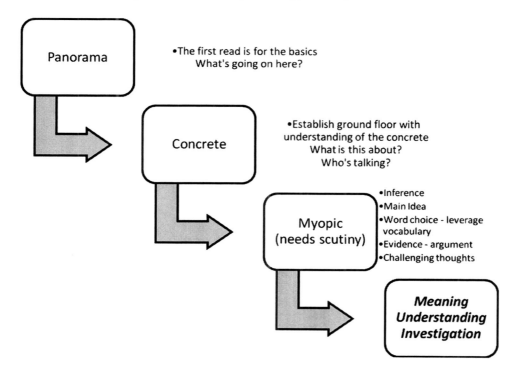

Brainstorm a TDQ for:	Text-dependent Questions
Panoramic Question	
Concrete question—basics	
Myopic question needing evidence	If this is about [subject], what is the message? What facts in this text support that main idea?
Myopic examination question	How is the word [xxxx] critical to this text's meaning?
Summary question for meaning	

Good TDQs will:

- **Move from concrete to abstract**
- **Cause students to search for meaning**
- **Guide the reader's understanding**
- **Support discovery**
- **Teach a student how to comprehend**
- **Spotlight standards**
- **Should not give away the answer, but cause the student to "discover" it**

Purposeful reading

As you read this book, contemplate your lesson plans and whether you are moving beyond rote and recall in your readalouds, your research endeavors, and your learning adventures. Every instructional minute can be carefully viewed as an opportunity to incubate higher level thought. TDQs are just the beginning. By nature, a TDQ wants students to carefully read and contemplate the content. A simple read-aloud can be transformed with critical TDQs to activate thinking and provide collaborative discussion or debate. In this book you will find a few readalouds turned into brain exercises.

CHAPTER 10

THINKING IN SOCIAL STUDIES

Young people need strong tools for, and methods of, clear and disciplined thinking in order to traverse successfully the worlds of college, career, and civic life.
National Council for the Social Studies, College, Career, and Civic Life C3 Framework
for Social Studies State Standards, 2013, p. 15

The National Council for the Social Studies, the CCSSO, the American Historical Association, and a prestigious collaborative of leading professional groups in the discipline have framed a new framework of standards in the social studies. The College, Career, and Civic Life C3 Framework for Social Studies State Standards 2013 sets up priorities for teachers that embrace thinking, key conceptual ideas, local choice about how to teach the key ideas in each grade, and a disciplinary structure that reinforces with ever-increasing complexity all important core concepts. Like the CCSS, these frameworks scaffold, extend, and build but hold to the central core. The essence of this document consists of big ideas developed over time, deep understanding, thinking, and decision making.

Thinking in social studies has a compass. That compass is discipline-specific, and it seeks true north in the interpretation of testimony of the past and present to approximate what really happened and why. Truth needs to be winnowed from testimony, records, perspectives, witnesses, biases, half-truths, partial truths, and truths that seemed to be true at one point but are no longer true at all. The compass is guided by disciplined expertise and those rich in content knowledge. Yet new, even declassified documentation continues to present itself. Swings in political attitudes popularize or file away important understandings. Decision making, key to the new frameworks, must be informed, yet the challenge to remain skeptical and validate can be daunting.

What does this mean for young learners who are still thinking apprentices? A compilation of guiding principles can be found in the Practices of Social Studies accepted by many educators in the field and incorporated into New York State's social studies frameworks draft. At each grade level thinking is vertically articulated and consistent. Learners demonstrate these practices with specific and observable performance targets.

Thinking in social studies integrates:

- Chronological thinking and causation
- Comparison and contextualization
- Geographic reasoning
- Gathering, using, and interpreting evidence
- The role of the individual in social and political interpretation

Lower Level Thinking in Social Studies	Higher Level Thinking in Social Studies
Describing	Gathering, using, citing evidence
Explaining	Distinguishing relevance, usefulness
Locating or recalling facts	Solving problems
Making lists	Applying concepts, transferring
Defining	Distinguishing discreet aspects of issues
Collecting, scrapbooking	Evaluating, recognizing misconceptions, validating
Comparing	Connecting a concept or theme across time
Categorizing, matching	Reasoning chronologically or geographically
Explaining cause and effect	Synthesizing from multiple sources
Explaining reasons	Interrogating and manipulating multiple perspectives
Identifying relationships	Developing arguments
Reciting	Using reason, logic, habits of mind
Summarizing	Judging by using criteria
Giving examples	Planning, producing, creating a new conclusion or perspective

A number of templates for thinking and cognitive rigor present a fairly unified picture of what lower level and higher level thinking look like in social studies. The Depth of Knowledge analysis of Norman L. Webb has been published by the CCSSO, the same organization that sparked the Common Core. *Smarter Balance* assessment guidance documents address cognitive rigor, as do Will Daggett and Karen Hesse. A common distinction of higher level thinking involves synthesis of multiple information sources and a learner who is actively engaged with a purpose. Other well-recognized matrices have common ground with these ideas regarding low level and high level thought in social studies:

CHAPTER 11

THINKING IN MATHEMATICS

Reasoning and sense making are simultaneously the purpose for learning mathematics and the most effective means of learning it. Unless students can reason with and make sense of the mathematics that they are learning, they are likely to ask the age-old question, "Why do we need to learn this?" They need to see a purpose in studying mathematics beyond the goal of preparing for the next mathematics course or standardized test. Moreover, research shows that students are more likely to retain mathematics that has its foundation in reasoning and sense making than mathematics that is presented as a list of isolated skills.

—National Council of Teachers of Mathematics

FOCUS IN HIGH SCHOOL MATHEMATICS: REASONING AND SENSE MAKING

The National Council of Teachers of Mathematics considers thinking about mathematics and thinking mathematically as equally important, if difficult to differentiate. Quality mathematical thinking encompasses the attributes of quality thinking in any discipline. Students who can explain math are thinking about math. Reasoning and sense making are at the heart of thinking in mathematics. Students who answer math questions or solve problems without thinking, reasoning, or sense making do not develop deep understanding. They forget their surface knowledge and do not retain. Test preparation and drill is soon forgotten, requiring teaching the same skill in the future. Eliciting thinking in math is key to the mastery of mathematics.

Mathematical thinking parallels scientific thinking in many ways. Learners identify and restate a problem. Learners analyze the problems and develop a hypothesis about solving them. They consider connections to concepts, other related problems, and evidence. They posit a solution and reflect on it. They test the solution and begin the cycle again.

Math tasks that involve memorization or that reproduce familiar steps fall require little thinking. The Trends in International Mathematics and Science Study (TIMSS) video analysis of math classrooms in the United States, Germany, and Japan provided evidence of contrasting priorities in the decades before the CCSS. The National Center for Educational Statistics continues to feature access to analysis of TIMSS video archives, as well as the outcomes of TIMSS test results. The TIMSS video documented the role of thinking and conceptual understanding in successful mathematical instruction and in a way heralded a new vision for the discipline.

Teachers in Japan involved learners in developing solutions to problems and put maximum value on thinking. Japanese teachers presented a problem, then encouraged learners to reflect on solutions and to suggest solutions. The goal of the teacher was the understanding of a concept. Students explained their reasoning and ultimately knew how the solution evolved. Parts of a lesson were linked to other parts

Lower Level Thinking in Math	Higher Level Thinking in Math
Recognizing	Explaining by using concepts
Recalling facts	Arguing the validity of a concept
Measuring	Explaining a concept
Following steps	Applying a concept
Reading charts, graphs	Defending an answer when many are possible
Charting data	Interpreting a graph or chart
Collecting	Selecting graphical information to use
Grouping, organizing	Comparing and contrasting
Making tables	Analyzing trends, predicting
Performing familiar function	Reasoning
Practicing a familiar procedure	Using concepts to solve, applying concepts over time
Finding a predictable solution	Deciding how to solve with options
Observing	Connecting with related problems, solutions, even other disciplines
Repeating steps	Synthesizing new understanding
Reproduce, copy	Evaluating and criticize, analyzing assumptions
Substitute	Solving with complex variables

of a lesson, connecting ideas and concepts. Further, Japanese students applied concepts and invented new solutions, clearly achieving a high level of thinking.

U.S. classroom video presented evidence of emphasis on practice of skills, stating rather than developing concepts, and using formulas. Lessons were often segmented, with many topics addressed in an isolated context. Teachers emphasized and reviewed homework and devoted a large proportion of classroom time to practicing examples of a concept that the teacher covered. Global competition for mathematical competency in the workforce prompted a shift with the CCSS.

The CCSS, with college and career readiness as the greatest priority, frames math standards that stress conceptual understanding, critical thinking, and the ability to apply math to real-world situations. Emphasizing math as the basis for well-founded decisions, the CCSS posits statistics and mathematical concepts as the basis for analysis in everyday life. Planning, evaluating, reflecting, organizing, and observing, as well as other features of expert thinking, are important in mathematical thinking. Rigorous math instruction builds in evidence-based argument for concepts and solutions to problems.

The new CCSS Standards in Mathematics use a brain-based approach to learning. Each year foundations are built for new learning the following year. A progression of conceptual understanding optimizes the sense of connections for the learner. Grade by grade, learners extend what they already know—prior knowledge—to develop new knowledge. Math, or any subject, as a long list of formidable topics defies long-term retention and coherence.

Analytical thinking and reasoning empowers learners to draw conclusions from data, compare and contrast ways of solving problems, and generalize. Synthesis caps mathematical thinking and is the catalyst for innovation, originality, and strategic solutions. Connecting ideas to relevant concepts in order to design models and conduct experiments demonstrates competence in mathematical thinking.

CHAPTER 12

THINKING IN SCIENCE

Outside a favorite spot where bear pancakes are served, a pint-sized toddler was stomping around on pieces of broken pavement. Attempting to piece the pavement chunks into the accompanying hole, he did a pretty good job of wedging them together. Brushing off his hands, he said to his mom, "Who broke it? Now tape it."

This is not exactly rocket science, but the very young brain was definitely thinking scientifically. Cause and effect, change over time, and problem solving were definitely observable, along with a little engineering. Scientific thinking is hard wired into the developing brain. Five-year-olds seek information, observe, and explore. Like real scientists, learners at an early age are very collaborative, share ideas, give feedback, and wrestle with problems. Children can manipulate and compare objects, describe, draw, and explain. They can use their experience to predict and draw conclusions about current situations, as evidenced when the budding Einstein wanted someone to tape the pavement. Understanding of life science, the environment, earth science, and meteorology grow from early curiosity and wonder.

A study published in 2010 called "Science in Early Childhood Classrooms: Content and Process," by Karen Worth, acknowledges the power of early thinking and learning, which was not previously recognized. Worth notes that science is a natural part of early learning, which is sparked by curiosity about the natural world. With this curiosity, children move forward and use inquiry to make sense of their world and develop a host of companion skills in the process.

AND NOW ON THE HORIZON

School librarians can certainly activate the scientific thinking at any age. A powerful new platform with meaningful connections for school librarians has arrived on the horizon: *A Framework for K–12 Science Education* and the *Next Generation Science Standards* (NGSS) merge brain-based learning standards with mathematics and ELA standards. True to the CCSS guidelines for scientific literacy, the NGSS frame lessons with *key concepts* and real-world scientific practices. Shifting from content coverage in science, these standards are designed for deep understanding. Here is the really good news: *Evidence-based claims, data-driven conclusions, and arguments based on evidence permeate the standards, which culminate in interdisciplinary performance tasks.* The writing and speaking standards address authentic real-world connections. This document has rich potential.

The National Research Council has recently addressed scientific learning and thinking in watershed books: *How Students Learn, Taking Science to School,* and *Education for Life and Work.* Findings in cognitive science characterize their *Framework for K–12 Science Education* and the *Next Generation Science Standards* (NGSS).

It is important to understand that the scientific practices in the Next Generation Science Standards (NGSS), as defined by the National Research Council (NRC), include the critical thinking and communication skills that students need for postsecondary success and citizenship in a world fueled by innovations in science and technology. These science practices encompass the habits and skills that scientists and engineers use day in and day out.

Next Generation Science Standards. http://www.nextgenscience.org/frequently asked questions. 21 April 2014.

The essence of scientific thinking is the quest for objective and provable truth. Unlike social studies, in which truth is reconstructed through testimony, secondary accounts, and perspectives, science is not science without fact. Levels of scientific thought reflect knowledge of scientific principle, the evaluation of evidence, and the verification of explanations. Inquiry is a process that integrates scientific thinking to such a degree that the two are indistinguishable in some disciplines. Again, critical thinking and information literacy come together. Inquiry and scientific thinking involve:

- Asking questions
- Planning and investigating
- Exploring and accessing information
- Analyzing information
- Evaluating information
- Organizing information
- Constructing meaning from information
- Drawing conclusions substantiated by data or facts; developing hypotheses
- Arguing using evidence
- Communicating information
- Reflecting
- Developing new questions

The scientific method parallels these steps and embodies critical thinking. At every level scientific thinking leads to objectivity, well-founded decisions, understanding of the invisible and visible world, and analytical habits of mind. Beginning with questions and wonder, scientific thinking and literacy is, in the words of Neil deGrasse Tyson, "the artery through which solutions for tomorrow's problems flow."

Low Level Thinking in Science	Higher Level Thinking in Science
Recalling a fact or a specific answer	Creating testable questions
Asking fact based questions	Perceiving relationships across texts or disciplines
Being aware of accuracy,	Organizing and analyzing data
Following a procedure, one step	Designing experiments, models
Using a familiar formula	Planning an investigation
Measuring, defining	Determining relevant and irrelevant information
Calculating	Distinguishing bias, incomplete information
Gathering data, charting, making a display	Evaluating for validity, precision, logic
Selecting useful facts	Self-assessing thinking
Categorizing	Interrogating point of view
Comparing and contrasting	Conceptualizing critically
Representing an idea in a picture	Interpreting
Reading a graph	Strategizing
Making sense of scientific texts	Drawing original conclusions
Writing a summary statement	Synthesizing
Observing properties	Solving problems with unpredictable outcomes
Recognizing a problem	Reasoning with evidence

From *Think Tank Library: Brain-Based Learning Plans for New Standards, Grades 6–12* by Mary Boyd Ratzer and Paige Jaeger. Santa Barbara, CA: Libraries Unlimited. Copyright © 2015.

CHAPTER 13

DEVELOPMENTAL SPOTLIGHT ON THINKING

THE PRIMARY GRADES: KINDERGARTEN THROUGH FIRST GRADE

Learners who are entering school have developed thinking skills. Integrating these skills into learning experiences and developing the level of the skills are keys to future performance and confidence. The brain-conscious teacher will carefully craft lessons to embrace skills as well as thought. Next . . .

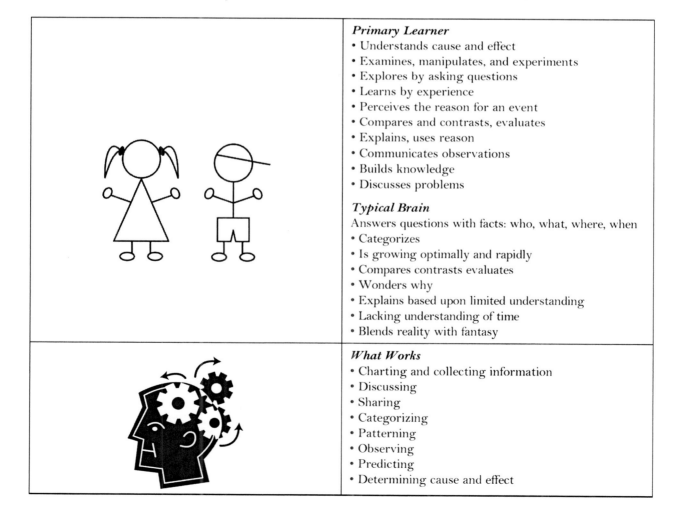

Primary Learner
- Understands cause and effect
- Examines, manipulates, and experiments
- Explores by asking questions
- Learns by experience
- Perceives the reason for an event
- Compares and contrasts, evaluates
- Explains, uses reason
- Communicates observations
- Builds knowledge
- Discusses problems

Typical Brain
Answers questions with facts: who, what, where, when
- Categorizes
- Is growing optimally and rapidly
- Compares contrasts evaluates
- Wonders why
- Explains based upon limited understanding
- Lacking understanding of time
- Blends reality with fantasy

What Works
- Charting and collecting information
- Discussing
- Sharing
- Categorizing
- Patterning
- Observing
- Predicting
- Determining cause and effect

LATE ELEMENTARY, EARLY MIDDLE SCHOOLERS

Learners in what is commonly called middle childhood develop a range of thinking skills, partly influenced by experience, formal instruction, interaction with adults and peers, as well as maturation. As they broaden and deepen their conceptual knowledge of the world around them, they expand their information processing capacity. Constructing more vigorous and adaptable conceptual understandings of the world, children begin to use these formative concepts with ease and reasonable speed. They expand these frameworks, and build their cognitive real estate. Working memory capacity expands. When this occurs, learners can begin to connect concepts and think in a more sophisticated way. Children make gains in the control of their attention, the ability to plan, and use thinking strategies. The CCSS specify developmentally appropriate progressions from grades 3 to 5 that teachers and librarians can use to make thinking skills their target skills.

Elementary Learner
- Understands cause and effect
- Reasoning based on facts and observations (details)
- Self-awareness about thinking and learning develops
- Confidence grows
- Thinking strategically grows
- Prior knowledge makes new knowledge easier to store in long-term memory

Typical Brain
- Metacognition becomes more sophisticated and productive and expands brain function and capacity
- Focus is increasingly key to performance in complex tasks, writing, and communicating
- Planning and goal setting evolve from amateur to apprentice
- Multiple causes and multiple effects can be understood and manipulated
- Immediate causes can be identified
- Long-term effects can be distinguished
- Change over time can be discerned and represented
- Relationships among patterns and processes are recognized
- Different forms of evidence are analyzed and used to construct meaning
- Inference begins and can be fostered by looking at relationships
- Expanding and structured networks in the brain facilitate retention of new knowledge
- Organization of mental tasks becomes faster and more extensively used
- Memory strategies begin to support new learning

What Works
- Chunking information
- Connecting information—concept mapping expands awareness and tracks learning
- Linking ideas within and across categories employs language that requires support for opinions
- Reasoning based on facts
- Requiring "evidence" to answer "why"
- Tools for self-assessment boost progress and performance
- Move questions from facts to *how, why, should,* and *what if*
- Starting requiring multiple perspectives to enhance understanding
- Integrating information from sources is increasingly based on evaluation of that information
- Making distinctions
- Logic in ordering ideas increasingly demands reflection and analysis
- Drawing conclusions from information and knowledge is genuine synthesis

EARLY ADOLESCENCE

Early adolescence is a time of critical brain growth. Early adolescent thinkers display the following characteristics:

Typical Brain
- Transition from concrete thinking to logical operations
- Develop abstract thinking and reasoning
- Store limited items in short-term memory at one time
- Develop the ability to combine related items and classify them
- Generalize
- Think creatively
- Begin to monitor and control thinking; plan
- Begin to reason deductively
- Begin to control impulses, coordinate thought and behavior
- Prefer active learning and peer interaction
- Infer and reason, drawing conclusions using thinking and not just experience
- Transition to framing possibilities as well as facts, ideas without actual objects
- Develop complex thinking and view of the world
- Express personal thoughts and views, have intense interests
- Focus on personal decision making, imagining outcomes of actions
- Calculate mathematically
- Solve problems
- Test variables in a systematic manner
- Question authority
- Move new learning into long-term memory when information connects with prior knowledge

What Works
- Chunking information
- Must be engaged for long-term retention of material
- Collaborative problem solving groups
- Infusing technology into delivery, collaboration, knowledge presentations
- Considering multiple perspectives of peers and others
- Starting to require multiple perspectives to enhance understanding
- Connecting information—concept mapping expands awareness and tracks learning
- Linking ideas within and across categories employs language that Requiring support for opinions
- Reasoning based on facts
- Requiring "evidence" to answer "why."
- Tools for self-assessment boost progress and performance
- Moving questions from facts to *how, why, should, what if*
- Integrating information from sources is increasingly based on evaluation of that information.
- Making distinctions
- Logic in ordering ideas increasingly demands reflection and analysis.
- Drawing conclusions from information and knowledge is genuine synthesis.

SPOTLIGHT ON THINKING: LATER ADOLESCENCE

As adolescence progresses, brain development refines and extends complex thinking skills. Practice with new capabilities generates increased confidence in the learner. Some thinking processes no longer demand effort and become familiar and automatic.

	***Typical Teen Brain*** • Grow in confidence as a thinker • Learn new thinking strategies • Use thinking strategies and modify them • Understand personal strengths or weaknesses • Grow in self-awareness and potential possibilities • Know that problems can be analyzed and solved • Think abstractly on an increasing scale • Plan long term and use thinking to make life decisions • Grow in core knowledge related to many disciplines • Transfer learning to new contexts • Question more consistently; question with a purpose • Consider global concepts such as human rights, social justice, and policy • Begin to frame ethical principles • Use distributed intelligence effectively in a social setting • Control, coordinate, and manage thinking • Grow in information processing skills • Synthesize multiple, complex texts to construct big ideas and conclusions • Use evidence to review beliefs and understandings • Develop knowledge by testing existing beliefs against new knowledge and revise or dismiss existing beliefs, if necessary • Identify the sources of their beliefs • Practice scientific thinking by investigating and analyzing evidence • Question the validity of inferences • Consider possibilities and generate alternatives • Reason and investigate to construct arguments • Validate thinking with reason • Defer to authority as the standard for truth • Take an absolutist stance, looking for one right answer • Can learn to reconcile opposing views when experts disagree • Progress beyond the standard of absolute certainty • Reconcile that opinions cannot be proven
	What Works Solving problems better with a social group • Developing knowledge based on evaluation and argument • Practicing with advanced conceptual knowledge • Drawing conclusions from multiple, quality information texts • Thinking about their own thinking, refining metacognition • Learning with challenges • Discussing possibilities • Debating correct paths and solutions, based upon evidence • Evaluating multiple perspectives and viewpoints • Synthesizing across texts, evidence, and viewpoints • Reasoning based on facts • Answering open-ended questions • Integrating information from sources is increasingly based on evaluation of that information • Defending why

CHAPTER 14

INTRODUCTION TO THINK-TANK LESSONS

When planning a lesson, we often weave expectations, learning targets, ideas, and details together in our mind knowing that they make sense. It is only when we have to write a lesson up for formal observation that we locate the district-approved lesson plan form and proceed to formally carve the lesson into pieces, scrutinizing the worthiness of each part so that we receive a favorable review. That same level of care and concern should now be front and center of all our lessons in order to optimize the use of time for student achievement. Remember—it's all about the kids.

Formal observation has moved beyond pieces fitting together in a delivery to asking, "What can my principal observe, not in my delivery, *but in the students*, to prove that I am an effective teacher"? These students behaviors are sometimes referred to as "dispositions." These dispositions are the evidence of student engagement, and student engagement is the secret to academic success. If the student is not engaged, the student will not learn.

The sample library-classroom lessons that follow are all aimed to optimize student engagement. All learning activities are intended to turn rote and recall upside down placing the student at the center of learning. Flip your lessons. Use these models to learn how students can do the learning, digging, investigating, brainstorming, and more. As you read these lessons, you will find repetitive pieces woven together to ensure your students are challenged to move to the top of Bloom's Taxonomy and beyond. These lessons are intended to embrace multiple CCSS shifts into each lesson thus exemplifying how the librarian can move beyond a simple read aloud to weaving together multiple goals of the CCSS to and become vital member of the instructional team.

Some of these lessons are intended to follow a classroom reading of a seed text. A seed text is intended to be a close reading activity that:

- Activates thinking on the curriculum content area
- Connects to prior knowledge
- Introduces a topic or a possible controversy within the topic
- Embeds the vocabulary of the discipline
- Poses two sides of an issue so that the issue requires an information investigation

The Common Core demands an integrated model of literacy throughout our instruction. Consider this quote from the standards:

Although the Standards are divided into Reading, Writing, Speaking and Listening, and Language strands for conceptual clarity, the processes of communication are closely connected, as reflected throughout.

With that in mind, the lessons which follow have been crafted to weave together reading, writing, speaking, and listening. These lessons demand rigor and relevance; embrace multiple instructional shifts; and optimize library instructional time. Our lessons examined other critical components such as the rigor of materials, to the integration of innovative assessment examples.

The national movement in assessment is to build in student self-assessment tools for empowerment. This places the responsibility squarely on the student to complete the task and also serves as a template for success. Both teacher and student can track progress with simple checklists. Self-assessment rubrics help to layout expectations for academic success.

In addition to detailed lesson templates, we have included "Think Tank Starter Kits." These are ideas for building your own rigorous, high-level thought unit. Pick and choose what you like and build bridges of collaboration with your colleagues.

ENGLISH LANGUAGE ARTS: LESSON PLANS AND THINK TANK STARTER KITS

Brand Yourself!   Brain-based Learning—Grade 9 ELA/Business

Jan Tunison, librarian, and Kelly Neiderer, English teacher, are a dynamic duo at the Scotia-Glenville High School, Scotia, New York. This duo enjoys designing new experiences for their students to develop their information fluency and English skills. All their learning experiences are authentic and real-world.

WHAT'S THE BIG IDEA BEHIND THE LESSON?

In 1997 Tom Peters wrote an article describing the concept of personal branding. He challenged readers with this quote, "We are CEOs of our own companies: Me Inc. To be in business today, our most important job is to be head marketer for the brand called "You."

Fast forward to contemporary times: While the branding concept is unfamiliar to students, they are experts on themselves, their actions, their activities, their hopes, and their dreams Students must brand themselves in face-to-face and digital environments for success in college and career ventures.

In this learning experience, students relate the branding concept to their lives. They consider the actions and inactions that contribute to their brand, and analyze the brand of an influential person for the purpose of strengthening their own. Students work with multiple sources; analyze text for fact, opinion, and bias; and synthesize information into a written branding improvement plan for the influential person and themselves. This experience requires students to search, research, struggle, think, take risks, make inferences, cite sources, and produce a written branding plan. Close reading and metacognition are key in this experience. In addition, the power of this learning experience is in co-teaching and making direct connection to students' lives.

Students use their knowledge of self to develop their own brand. Subsequently, students work through the *non-googleable* experience of analyzing the brand of an influential person using multiple sources and creating an improvement plan for the brand of the influential person.

Through this process, students discover that a person may develop a *public* and a *private* brand. They also incorporate the use of social media to study the person's brand. Due to breadth of cognitive levels in grade 9 students, this learning experience is recommended as a co-teaching experience.

This unit can end with a showcase of brands: The Best in Branding! Guess who is who.

Students finishing early can be challenged to create brands for historical figures, scientists, or current newsmakers. Students can give "upgrades" to celebrities or politicians and craft "makeovers" for newsmakers needing an "upgrade."

Lesson:	Brand Yourself! And... Branding Upgrades!
Learning targets	Students will examine themselves and craft a "brand" to represent who they are. Students will understand the impact of media. Students will synthesize who they are into a personal representation. Students will research to understand how branding has impacted marketing. Students will examine "newsmakers" and frame a branding makeover.

Essential questions	How do I (student) want to be perceived? How do people currently perceive me (student)? What are the steps that I need to take to build my own brand (student)? Why should I care about the brand called Me?				
Text	**Possible texts:** "The power of branding." *Design Council*. N.p., n.d. Web. 6 June 2014. <http://www.designcouncil.org.uk/news-opinion/power-branding> DiPaulo, Christine, and others. "iAm." *iTunes*. N.p., n.d. Web. 15 Apr. 2014. <https://itunes.apple.com/us/itunes-u/iam/id492587276?mt=10>. "Full List: The World's 100 Most Influential People | TIME.com." *TIME.com*. N.p., n.d. Web. 15 Apr. 2014. Singer, Natasha. "They Loved Your G.P.A. Then They Saw Your Tweets." *The New York Times*, 9 Nov. 2013. Web. 15 Apr. 2014. Suggestion for independent reading titles could include *So Yesterday*, by Scott Westervelt. Although the Lexile level is too low for this instructional level, this makes a good choice for outside reading as it has a branding theme amid mystery.				
Power words	Acuity, Brand or Branding, Bias, CEO, Fact, Opinion, Perceive or Perception Resume or ResuME (see DiPaulo) Any academic words extracted from the seed texts chosen, such as these from the NYT article: covertly, peruse, elucidation, obscure, etc.				
Vocabulary of library discipline	Research, depth of knowledge, synthesis, correlation, narrow, broaden, keywords, bias, credible, accurate, reliable, sources				
CCSS goals	x	Vocabulary use	x	Solve real-world issues	x	Discuss, interpret, explain
	x	Nonfiction use	x	Research	x	Use formal English
	x	Close reading	x	Build and present knowledge	x	Rigor
	x	Evidence-based claim			x	Relevance
Rigor	After a close reading activity, students should be challenged to embrace the academic vocabulary of the seed text to improve their brain. The rigor of this lesson is asking students to look introspectively and examine their hearts. In a world of tabloid journalism and surface relationships, it is hard to think deeply. As students enter high school, this is an activity which may help shape their direction for the next four years. By researching influential people and finding how they are represented with reputations, one-word identities, and legacies, students should be challenged to synthesize history and reality.				

Relevance	Relevance couldn't be more timely. Most seniors are trying to figure out who they are and what they want to do with the rest of their life. This helps take a few steps in that direction.
Reader and the task	After reading and researching how famous people have identified themselves by what they've accomplished, who they are, what they are known for, and what others have said about them, students can start to identify what people think of them, what defines them, how they want to describe themselves, and more.
Assessment	Pre-assessment: Who are you? Post-assessment: What's your Brand Me? Writing task: A short written persuasive script for an NPR infomercial on your chosen influential person. In one minute or less, inform the world of your newsmaker, using branding words and evidence from research, and personify what they stand for. Sum it up with a slogan or choice word. Brand them. Record the infomercial via technology of your choice.
Think tank spotlight	• Develop abstract thinking and reasoning • Use reason, logic, habits of mind • Evaluate, recognize misconceptions, validate • Plan, produce, create a new conclusion or perspective • Distinguish relevance, usefulness • Think creatively • Begin to monitor and control thinking, plan • Begin to reason deductively, and think ethically • Prefer active learning and peer interaction • Infer and reason • Solve problems
Standards spotlight	**Common Core Standards:** • Integrate and evaluate multiple sources of information presented in diverse formats and media (e.g., visually and quantitatively, as well as in words) in order to address a question or solve a problem • Research to build and present knowledge • Conduct short research projects to answer a question • Narrow or broaden your search • Synthesize and demonstrate understanding of the topic • Avoid plagiarism • Develop the idea with well-chosen relevant facts • Cite your sources [© Copyright 2010. National Governors Association Center for Best Practices and Council of Chief State School Officers. All rights reserved.]

Bloom's barometer	Remembering	Understanding	Applying	Analyzing	Evaluating	Creating
		X	X	X	X	x

From *Think Tank Library: Brain-Based Learning Plans for New Standards, Grades 6–12* by Mary Boyd Ratzer and Paige Jaeger. Santa Barbara, CA: Libraries Unlimited. Copyright © 2015.

Think About	The Brand Called Me
What do you value?	
What's your vision?	
What's your passion?	
What do you do well?	
What are four words describing you? (Use a thesaurus to get ideas)	
Synthesize Brainstorm Big Idea Clarity	
Sloganizer.net Use your ID words to brainstorm possible slogans- pay attention to sentiment and tone of voice	

Dystopian Literature as a Catalyst for Social Action   Grade 9

WHAT'S THE BIG IDEA?

Through transparent thinking, peer review, Socratic seminar, and reflection, this lesson will:

* Transform passive readers to active thinkers.
* Transform active thinkers into communicators who take action and address a humanitarian crisis.
* Inform new and better strategic thinking.
* Raise the level of engagement.

Works of fiction have been mirrors of the human experience for centuries. While creating a dystopian fictional world, authors shine a critical light on the human actions, ethical principles, injustice, and oppression. Classic works of science fiction generate sweeping questions about who we are as humans, our potential to benefit or destroy, our wisdom, and our blindness.

Grade 9 learners, capable of abstract thought and ethical decision making, can read a dystopian novel of their choice. For years, *Lord of the Flies* by William Golding has been read, but students could be given similar current dystopian choices. They can discuss subjective and personal meaning, along with thematic elements and the interplay of characters, with careful and explicit analysis of text. An important background piece would be understanding the geopolitical realities of the time in which the book is written or that could be in the future.

Just as transparent thinking and discussion uncovers Golding's perspective on human nature and its consequences, discussion can embrace similar themes in their dystopian novel. Response from the readers can generate conclusions about the relevance of the novels in the world today.

Students will investigate a humanitarian crisis that is compelling and can brainstorm and map connections between the dystopia and our real-world. Any crisis can be chosen from as close as their own family, classroom, government, or community to one or another continent. Their choice must be justified, and understood. They will decide on a personal response that they can make to the crisis, persuade others to join them in action, and use technology to communicate.

A research question or thesis will be developed through background reading and analysis. Peers, teachers, and librarians will engage in Socratic seminars that interrogate issues, perspectives, convictions, evidence, and action.

Students will conduct background building research on the crisis, evaluating information sources for authority. Using their own voice and creative power, students will take a position on the injustice, oppression, or violation of rights. Supporting their position with evidence, students will communicate persuasively regarding the need to resolve the crisis, the harmful impacts, agents and strategies for resolution, and personal actions that can impact awareness. Artistic expression, poetry, visual media, and web-based communication can be the platform for increasing awareness and persuasion as they present their knowledge product.

Lesson:	Literature as a Catalyst for Social Action—Grade 9		
Learning targets: This lesson uses standards from the Empire State Information Fluency Continuum and shows how you can embrace any local standard(s) to ensure alignment.	Reads to solve problems Reads to explore ideas Reads background information to discover the complexities of the problem Brainstorms ideas for further inquiry Uses multiple resources Seeks a balanced and global perspective Focuses on the purpose of research by formulating specific questions Determines the kind of information needed to investigate the complexities Examines multiple perspectives Uses search strategies to broaden and narrow searches Locates appropriate resources Uses technology resources such as the online catalogs, encyclopedias, databases, and valid websites to locate primary and secondary information Takes notes using one or more of a variety of note-taking strategies Combines ideas and information to develop new understanding Organizes information independently—analyzing relationships among ideas and general patterns Understands and builds on the ideas of others Presents conclusions to answer the question or problem Uses visuals, electronic tools, and multimedia to communicate meaning Expresses own ideas creatively		
Essential questions:	How can dystopian literature serve as a catalyst for social action? How can informed, individual action be a catalyst for needed change? How does literature reflect real-life issues?		
Text	*Lord of the Flies* by William Golding or other modern dystopian novels of student's choice such as: *The House of the Scorpion* by Nancy Farmer *Matched* by Allie Condie *Clockwork Orange* by Anthony Burgess *Divergent* by Veronica Roth *All* these novels have Lexiles below the CCSS recommended level for instructional purposes. Some are "canonized." It is interesting to note that even some classic ELA novels fall below CCSS rigor expectations. When a classic novel measures as an easy read, it is important for instructors to include rigorous tasks to justify instructional use. The vocabulary in Golding's book easily justifies its use as noted below by a handful of academic vocabulary words. Visit Vocabulary.com and search for your book's power words. Other nonfiction, authoritative informational sources in multiple formats as encountered during research:		
Power words	Antagonism Appall Balm Belligerence Chastisement Contemptuously	Enmity Exhilaration Furtive Immure Impalpable Incredulous	Myriad Officious Pallor Pliant Recrimination Strident

From *Think Tank Library: Brain-Based Learning Plans for New Standards, Grades 6–12* by Mary Boyd Ratzer and Paige Jaeger. Santa Barbara, CA: Libraries Unlimited. Copyright © 2015.

	Contrite Decorous Dubious Ebullience Effulgence		Incursion Interpose Loll Mortification		Susurration Swath Vagrant Vicissitude (and others...)	
Vocabulary of library discipline	Narrow or broaden topic, cite textual evidence, plagiarism, synthesis, verify, multiple formats, authority, audience, personal voice, close reading, theme, dystopia, inquiry, primary and secondary, research question, thesis					
CCSS objectives	Nonfiction Use	x	Research	x	Use formal English	x
	Close reading	x	Build and present knowledge	x	Relevance	x
	Evidence-based claim	x	Building knowledge across the discipline	x	Rigor	x
Rigor	The literary work *Lord of the Flies* has a Lexile of 770 but a significantly higher difficulty factor due to archaic language, allusions to different worlds, and use of British English. (Even the dystopian Pulitzer Prize winning book *The Road* has a low Lexile.) Vocabulary is challenging but sentence length is fairly short, and the main characters are children. Learners in grade 9 have the moral, conceptual, and comprehension capacity to understand the thematic aspects of this work against a historical background. The unit has many rigorous elements, the most important of which is authentic development of a high-level question, or thesis, regarding a humanitarian crisis. A surface understanding of a crisis is deepened by: • The use of Socratic seminars and peer review to discuss issues in the novel • The reflection and refining of a personally relevant issue, understood in depth • Generating a question for investigation using multiple informational texts • Synthesis of these texts to draw conclusions • The organization of main ideas and details to communicate effectively and persuasively • Using technology to communicate to a real-world audience creatively					
Relevance	Relevance is the single strongest force to move a novel read in an ELA class beyond an empty required task which emphasizes chapter tests for comprehension and vocabulary quizzes. Lifting the experience of a classic dystopian novel to a meaningful and thoughtful inquiry is only possible with relevance to the learner and the immediate world. Can Golding speak to each learner in thematic meaning, character development, and fictional premise? Can Golding be taken to the level of personal meaning prompting social action in response to a humanitarian crisis in the world of the 21st century? Motivating a ninth grader to get beyond the *selfie* and the novel for homework, one chapter at a time, cannot occur without real-world connections and the expectation					

	that meaning can and will drive personal commitment and communication. A choice of a humanitarian crisis, close to home or halfway across the globe, needs to resonate with the learner after background building. Relevance in this unit is highly personal where choice drives the research component. Socratic seminars bring to the surface a purpose for learning, reasons for a research question, and a substantial rationale for pursuing a topic. Discernment of deep understanding occurs through the quality of a thesis, the student's use of verifiable evidence, representative data, visuals, expert analysis, and impact. Therein lies the litmus test for relevance versus lip service.
Reader and the task	In reading the text as well as research nonfiction materials, students will link literature to real life while they build an "action plan for change." This action plan becomes the "task" which the Common Core requires. Students will build evidence-based claims and embrace all *Writing for Information Standards* of the Common Core through their knowledge product. We recommend the use of student-centered blogs, with required postings per text chapter to reflect on real-life issues mirrored in the book. The summative knowledge product will be a written paper supporting their claim and public service announcements may come in the form of technology products of the student's choice.
Assessment	Student blog postings will assess whether reading is on target. See the Thinking Rubric for summative assessment of knowledge product communicating persuasively regarding a humanitarian crisis and personal action. Emphasize critical thinking and conceptual understanding of content concepts and issues. Graphic organizer samples follow. Use these to assess whether your students are on track. Gathering an Understanding Chart will help your students gather and connect background knowledge to frame an inquiry. A Synthesis Chart will help them organize, conclude, and synthesize information to frame the main idea and supporting details. Create a checklist for effective use of a digital platform to communicate to a meaningful audience effectively considering task, purpose, and audience. Peer review, conferencing, and feedback for Socratic seminars and discussion of literature using a rubric.
Think tank spotlight	• Need practice with advanced conceptual knowledge • Begin to frame a set of ethical principals • Solve problems better with a social group • Think about their own thinking, refining metacognition with experience • Know that problems can be analyzed and solved • Think abstractly on an increasing scale • Synthesize multiple complex texts to construct big ideas and conclusions • Draw conclusions from multiple quality-information texts • Develop knowledge by testing existing beliefs against new knowledge • Reach understandings that revise or dismiss existing beliefs • Use evidence to review beliefs and understandings; debate

	• Identify the sources of their beliefs • Question the validity of inferences • Validate thinking with reason • Consider possibilities and generate alternatives • Reason and investigate to construct arguments
Standards spotlight	**Common Core:** • Write informative/explanatory texts to examine and convey complex ideas. • Develop the topic with well-chosen, relevant, and sufficient facts. • Conduct short as well as more sustained research projects to answer a question (including a self-generated question); solve a problem; narrow or broaden the inquiry when appropriate; synthesize multiple sources on the subject, demonstrating understanding of the subject under investigation. • Gather relevant information from multiple authoritative print and digital sources, using advanced searches effectively; assess the usefulness of each source in answering the research question; integrate information into the text selectively to maintain the flow of ideas, avoiding plagiarism, and following a standard format for citation. • Use technology, including the Internet, to produce, publish, and update individual or shared writing products. • Cite strong and thorough textual evidence to support analysis of what the text says explicitly as well as inferences drawn from the text. • Determine a theme or central idea of a text and analyze in detail its development over the course of the text. [© Copyright 2010. National Governors Association Center for Best Practices and Council of Chief State School Officers. All rights reserved.]

Bloom's barometer	Remembering	Understanding	Applying	Analyzing	Evaluating	Creating
	x	x	x	x	x	x

GATHERING AN UNDERSTANDING

Read background information to build an understanding and find something interesting.

Use this chart to reflect on whether a source provides general information as an overview or detailed information for deep discovery.

Source:		
Criteria	**Look for:**	**Your thoughts:**
General informal overview:	• Focused on big idea, not specific examples • General encyclopedia article • Summary statements	
Attention to topic details?	• Table of contents • Many chapters • Index • Navigation hyperlinks, if online	
CARS?	• Is copyright date current enough for the topic? • Accuracy—includes data and examples of evidence • Reliable—seems to match other information and from a note-worthy source • Supported—does this agree with other information read?	

Main ideas I knew before that were confirmed:

-
-
-
-

Ideas and interests from the text: (Don't copy; bullet your thoughts for further investigation)

-
-
-
-

Synthesis Chart	Organize your information through the "lenses" on the left. Analyze, group, and sort to help you conclude and synthesize meaning to answer your question or thesis.
Similarities?	
Cause and effect?	
Chronology?	
Is there a pattern?	
Group them from most important to least	
Which facts help me answer my thesis the best?	
Main idea facts	
Supporting detail facts	

Thinking Rubric: How well did you conclude and organize your thoughts?				
Evaluate:	**Great!** Clear and supported	**Good** Stated but lacks support Present but not strong	**Not yet or fuzzy** Consider this again	**Missing** Let's talk
Strong claim				
Supported by evidence				
Identified relationships or patterns				
Good transitions and linking thoughts				
Evidence presented in logical order				
Conclusions based on evidence				
Demonstrates deep understanding of the issue and uses vocabulary of the discipline				

HOW THE OTHER HALF LIVES, BY JACOB RIIS

Active and Responsible Citizens Emulating 19th Century Social Reform

The Big Idea: Grade 8 Social Studies/ELA

"Active and responsible citizens identify and analyze public problems; deliberate with other people about how to define and address issues; take constructive, collaborative action; reflect on their actions; create and sustain groups; and influence institutions both large and small."

> National Council for the Social Studies (NCSS), The College, Career, and Civic Life (C3)
> Framework for Social Studies State Standards, p. 19.

Primary documents from history open a portal into the past allowing us to view history through the perspective of those who create records of events, places, people, and problems. Often that record generated action in its own time, as did the watershed study of poverty in the tenements of New York City in the late 19th century, *How the Other Half Lives.*

Addressing the plight of almost half the residents of New York in 1890, Riis incorporated his disturbing photographs of tenement life and data from Dr. Roger S. Tracy, Registrar of Vital Statistics in the City of New York. Riis wanted action from the city to change its ineffectual laws governing living conditions of the poor. He urged private enterprise to provide funding to remodel existing tenements or build new ones. Jacob Riis lived the premise that active and responsible citizens define and address issues. As a respected journalist, he published a record of misery and hopeless poverty for all to witness. He took constructive action. He sparked change. The Progressive Era in U.S. history went forward with reform because of the documentation and action of reformers like Riis.

Exploring the archive of Jacob Riis's photographs and text selections from *How the Other Half Lives,* grade 8 social studies students will embark on a learning experience. They will deeply analyze Riis's motivation, perspective, and evidence through his writing and photography. Background building will reach out across time to briefly uncover related exemplars in history. Examples from other times and places include the work of photographer Dorothea Lange, who captured the plight of migrant farmers during the Dust Bowl, and texts of the muckrakers. A possible companion work of fiction, set in the tenements, is *A Tree Grows in Brooklyn* by Betty Smith.

The College, Career, and Civic Life (C3) Framework for Social Studies State Standards and the CCSS standards unify the lesson. The CCSS Reading for Information and Writing standards for grade 8 define the final product in this lesson. That product is an evidence-based argument for social reform in the present, in the school, the community, state, or world. Students will convey an argument with visual, statistical, and written evidence from primary and secondary sources. A focus on poverty, human suffering, and human need will parallel the historical documents. The inquiry process will frame the lesson with critical thinking key in developing questions, focusing on a proposed reform, interrogating perspectives, investigation for evidence, synthesis into a multimedia product, and communicating that product to bring about real-world change.

Lesson:	Active and Responsible Citizens Emulating 19th Century Social Reform and Jacob Riis's *How the Other Half Lives*—Grade 8 Social Studies/ELA
Learning targets:	Learners will study the effects of poverty on humanity and meet these standards: C3 Social Studies Framework: • Analyze how people's perspectives influenced what information is available in the historical sources they created • Use questions generated about multiple historical sources to identify further areas of inquiry and additional sources • Evaluate the relevancy and utility of a historical source based on information such as maker, date, place of origin, intended audience, and purpose CCSS: • Cite specific textual evidence to support analysis of primary and secondary sources. • Write arguments to support claims with clear reasons and relevant evidence
Essential questions:	How can communicating with authority the realities of human suffering be a first step to social reform?
Guiding questions:	Why did Jacob Riis and other reformers use data, images, and descriptive detail to convey human need? How did Jacob Riis's book *How the Other Half Lives* spark the conscience of a nation of rich and poor and serve as a catalyst for social reform? How could social reform address the division of wealth in America today? Why are we a nation of haves and have-nots? How can the individual communicate the realities of hopeless human suffering today?
Text and images	Selected close reading of texts from: Jacob A Riis (1849–1914), *How the Other Half Lives*, 1890. Chapter VI. The Bend Chapter XV. The Problem of the Children Chapter XXV. How the Case Stands Illustrations & Quotes: Bartleby.com/208/ or Google Books Selected photographs from the Library of Congress exhibit of Dorothea Lange and migrant workers from the Dust Bowl. Texts from the economist Paul Taylor, "The Forgotten People," American Memory Archive http://www.loc.gov/exhibits/treasures/trm016.html Selected archives and texts from Library of Congress: "The Muckrakers" http://www.loc.gov/exhibits/treasures/trm140.html *A Tree Grows in Brooklyn* by Betty Smith The Economic Bill of Rights, inaugural address, President Roosevelt

Power words	Social reform, journalist, tenements, tenants, incessant, death rate, truant officer, incessantly, transformation, immigrant, waif, abominations, servitude, rag picker, offal, undertaker, vital statistics, stand point, reform, landlord, influx, hovel, luxurious, exposure, indefinitely, starvation, urban, suburban					
Vocabulary of library discipline	Evidence-based claim, analyze, evaluate, synthesize, multiple perspectives, primary documents, secondary documents, relevance, inquiry, intended audience, critical thinking					
CCSS objectives	x	Vocabulary use	x	Solve real-world issues	x	Discuss, interpret, explain
	x	Nonfiction use	x	Research	x	Use formal English
	x	Close reading	x	Build and present knowledge	x	Rigor
	x	Evidence-based claim	x	Text-based answers	x	Relevance
Rigor	The primary text of *How the Other Half Lives* is written in 19th century journalistic style with a steep vocabulary, historical and geographical allusions, and statistical data from the time period. Analysis is densely illustrated with close-up vignettes, schematics, and persuasive appeal for empathy. Sorting out these elements and managing them in regard to fact and opinion is rigorous. Reconstructing historical realities from multiple perspectives is rigorous. Further transferring both communication strategies and broad subject area to today's real-world is rigorous. Writing an evidence-based claim deeply rooted in the need for contemporary social reform demands proof of understanding on multiple levels, including synthesizing multiple sources and demonstrating empathy. Rigor also characterizes the shared communication of a claim with visual enhancement. The fiction book *A Tree Grows in Brooklyn* is grade-level appropriate but uses a historical setting requiring background building.					
Relevance	The eighth-grade student is ready to develop an ethical perspective and think about history across a broad spectrum of time and place. The shocking realities of New York's tenements in 1890 surely parallel the plight of forgotten people in a world divided by an increasingly polarized distribution of wealth. A recent book called *The Plutocrats* compares the 21st century in America to the Gilded Age. Finding connections to human deprivation and need in the student's world, and addressing that need as an agent of change, is highly relevant. This lesson will move the camera on the smartphone of life from the teen to the larger world, drastically broadening perspective.					

Reader and the task	Close reading of selected rigorous primary documents will require background building, tapping of prior knowledge, and vocabulary instruction. Readers can code text and identify unfamiliar words. A Word Wall constructed by readers can facilitate mastering the vocabulary necessary for comprehension.
	Guiding questions and the essential question can frame the reading and viewing of multiple primary sources. Generating deep understanding of multiple perspectives, this reading will be accompanied by discussion, journaling, Socratic questioning, and concept mapping. Big ideas will be generated that pervade all aspects of the lesson.
	Consideration of journalistic style, the motivation of the writer, and his purpose and audience will engage students in a model for their own writing of an evidence-based argument for social reform.
Assessment	**Formative:** Reader response in journal entries, mind mapping, discussion, and use of graphic organizers for evidence-based claims- Students use "Claim and Evidence" graphic organizer (Appendix) **Summative:** Evidence-Based Claims Graphic Organizers In addition, please see the graphic organizers in this book's appendix. (Odell Education.com has a goldmine of valuable graphic organizers for research. These include rubrics, planners, and more. These can be found at: http://odelleducation.com/literacy-curriculum)
Think tank spotlight	• Transition from concrete thinking to logical operations • Develop abstract thinking and reasoning • Synthesize from multiple sources • Distinguish discreet aspects of issues • Interrogate and manipulate multiple perspectives • Connect a concept or theme across time • Gather, use, cite evidence • Developing arguments • Use reason, logic, habits of mind • Evaluate, recognize misconceptions, validate • Reason chronologically or geographically • Plan, produce, create a new conclusion or perspective • Distinguishing relevance, usefulness • Think creatively • Begin to monitor and control thinking, plan • Begin to reason deductively, and think ethically • Prefer active learning and peer interaction • Infer and reason, drawing conclusions using thinking and not just experience • Solve problems • Move new learning into long-term memory when information connects with prior knowledge

Standards spotlight	**Common Core** • Write arguments to support claims with clear reasons and relevant evidence. • Use precise language and domain-specific vocabulary to inform about or explain the topic. • Cite specific textual evidence to support analysis of primary and secondary sources. • Determine the central ideas or information of a primary or secondary source; provide an accurate summary of the source distinct from prior knowledge or opinions. • Integrate visual information (e.g., in charts, graphs, photographs, videos, or maps) with other information in print and digital texts. • Distinguish among fact, opinion, and reasoned judgment in a text. • Analyze the relationship between a primary and secondary source on the same topic. **C3—Standards for College, Career, and Civic Life** • Analyze how people's perspectives influenced what information is available in the historical sources they created. • Use questions generated about multiple historical sources to identify further areas of inquiry and additional sources. • Evaluate the relevancy and utility of a historical source based on information, such as maker, date, place of origin, intended audience, and purpose. • Explain multiple causes and effects of events and developments in the past. [© Copyright 2010. National Governors Association Center for Best Practices and Council of Chief State School Officers. All rights reserved.]

STARTER KITS FOR ENGLISH LANGUAGE ARTS

Time to Launch Lessons for your Brain-Friendly Library!

Additional ideas are listed below to inspire you to build your own inquiry-based learning endeavor with your teachers. Having read this book, you are likely equipped to develop deep student-centered learning endeavors from the ideas below.

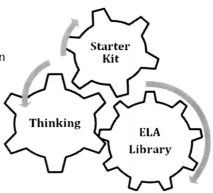

Text or Content	Inquiry Lesson in English Language Arts
Memoirs in fewer than ten words **Tweet the essence!**	**EQ: How can six or seven words capture the essence of a human life experience?** Acadia Middle School, Clifton Park, New York, created a hybrid research and writing lesson based on popular publications like *Smith* magazine and Internet repositories of six or seven words memoirs. The New York Public Library (NPR), and Smith's Twitter account ignited wide interest in the intense and precise craft of summing up a life experience in a few powerful words. Eventually several compilations of these memoirs were published in a series by Harper Perennial. School librarian Ann Samuelson shared the power of this experience and the enthusiasm of the students involved. With their emerging sense of personal identity, and the importance of inspiring role models, learners used texts to build understanding of a person that inspires them. Using details only to inform big ideas about that person, students write and share memoirs in fewer than ten words, words that distill the essence of their person from the perspective of the writer. This could be seen as an ultimate synthesis of authentic and relevant non-fiction.
Never cry wolf!	**EQ: Should wolves be reintroduced into the [your local wild]?** This classic nonfiction narrative read is still engaging for today's millennials. What would you do if the government dropped you off in the wild to study wolves and then forgot about you? With this engaging scenario, students are challenged with a thought that brings relevance to the reading. This short, captivating nonfiction book is full of academic vocabulary and is an appropriately Lexiled novel for high school. Follow this read with a short research investigation on wolves in order to prepare for a debate. Should wolves be reintroduced into a national, state, or local park? Students can choose sides and speak with evidence. Use the discussion rubric provided earlier in the Bill of Rights lesson. Invite local conservation officials in to moderate the discussion or debate and contribute their thoughts.

Social reform in the 1800s? *Jane Eyre* by **Charlotte Bronte and social reform: Socratic seminars**	**EQ: How was the novel *Jane Eyre* by Charlotte Bronte a catalyst for social reform in early 19th century England?** Students read and discuss *Jane Eyre* with the purpose of understanding many aspects of early 19th century life, and they build background knowledge by exploring areas of interest. Roles and rights of women, treatment of the mentally ill, property ownership and inheritance, the welfare of the poor, and education highlight the topics chosen for investigation. Background building also focuses on the author, her personal and artistic life, and literary contemporaries who also sparked social reform. **Texts** An extensive literary criticism collection, including the series *Nineteen Century Literary Criticism*, compiled essays in works like Bloom's *Modern Critical Interpretations, The Mad Woman in the Attic*, the database Twaynes Authors, and journal articles on Electric Library and Proquest Platinum, provided the foundation for research and analysis. Teams of students worked together to research and synthesize authoritative sources. The high school library becomes base camp for the climb to insight and deep understanding. Students as workers spend their classes collaborating and researching. Their teacher, in a conference room adjoining the literary criticism collection, coaches teams for their seminars, and finally conducts the seminars. Groups choose an area of social reform to address in Socratic seminars apropos the novel. Melding critical analysis with historic accounts of conditions and human rights, the students prepare for Socratic seminars where they would address probing questions and defend their conclusions with textual evidence. In a climate of critical engagement, students demonstrate depth of knowledge, original thinking, and understanding. This lesson originated in Shenendehowa Senior High School, Clifton Park, New York, and was designed by English teacher Wendy Jacques for 11th graders.
Parting words	**EQ: How can seniors change their community by mentoring middle school students?** In a dramatic turn from the senior research paper, students who are about to graduate use journals to capture life experience in the school and community. In candid discussions, seniors brainstorm key issues that are relevant and meaningful. Conducting an Internet search, they investigate an issue of their choice, determine the local connection, and generate a product that can be shared with middle school students as parting words. The products can be personal messages, visual infographics, a practical guide to surviving high school, an open letter, a presentation, a dramatic role play for an assembly or class, a song, or a banner. The criteria for the product include real-world relevance, research-based content, and effective communication to middle school students who will be entering high school as seniors are leaving. The lesson breaks through senioritis, branches out beyond the classroom, unifies the school community, and makes a difference.
Oppression doesn't stop or start with the Holocaust **Ubuntu!**	**EQ: How does man's inhumanity to man persist over time and geographic boundaries?** Students who read *Night* by Ellie Wiesel and parts of Victor Frankel's *Man's Search for Meaning* engage in research about an incidence of inhumanity and oppression. A middle school choice of a mentor text might be *Sold* by Patricia McCormick. Students use a background building process to focus on a specific violation of human rights.

	Some examples include the genocides in Sudan, Rwanda, Cambodia, or Albania; the plight of children sold into slavery in Bangladesh; the capture or killing of girls in schools in Afghanistan or Nigeria; South Africa's Apartheid; child labor in Asia; victimization of African Americans in Rosewood, Florida; or the war against Native Americans in the 19th century. Using databases that address the subject of human rights, students explore possible options. They investigate and read significant, related, primary texts, literary texts, and information texts. Students extend their understanding beyond the original mentor text. Using nonfiction information sources, students analyze the inhumanity, its perpetrators, its victims, and its underlying causes. The final product incorporates new knowledge and understanding of specific oppression in the world. Students collaboratively discuss, synthesize, and create media-based projects in which the common ground of man's inhumanity to man is distilled. Visual, photographic, musical, poetic, narrative, and dramatic expression is generated and shared in an iMovie, MovieMaker, or other multimedia choice with community audiences. The theme of the composite media is the South African word for respect, which also means humanity toward others: Ubuntu.
Middle School variation on oppression lesson: Let's solve a problem!	**EQ: How can students solve the problem of intolerance, hate, and abuse in their immediate world?** In reading circles, students read a choice of YA fiction that deals with bullying, mean girls, peer-to-peer abuse, hate speech, harassment, and interpersonal violence. Students analyze their novel in the light of the actions of characters, the central problem, and possible solutions. **Possible text choices** There are many novels on bullying, but most are not correctly Lexiled for a secondary instructional level. In fact, most have a readability suited for grades where the content is not appropriate such as Lexile 600—a third-grade level. These two novels weigh in appropriately for middle school: *The Chosen* by Chaim Potok (Lexile 970) *The Misfits* by James Howe (Lexile 960) Open-ended questions about problems can be generated from a concept mapping exercise using events in the novel. Students share their real-world concerns and choose an area to research. Through journaling, students can record real-life observations from their school or community. Using quality informational texts and databases, along with bullying case studies, students investigate and develop understanding about the problem portrayed in fiction. The focus of their research is how other communities and schools found solutions for problems. In teams, students prepare research-based (persuasive) public service announcements (PSAs) for their school that present solutions, choices, action, and rationale for change. These PSAs can be visual, written, dramatic, animated, or digital. Personal agency is a powerful motivator for middle school students. Learners discover the power of self-expression and authentic research in solving relevant problems.

Biography makeover: What indelible footprints did your person leave behind?	**EQ: What indelible footprint did your person leave on our world?** **EQ: How did our person influence the world for good or evil?** **EQ: What would the world be like, had this person not walked the planet?** Biographies are the most scammed reports on the planet. We have to transform biography reports to withstand the Google litmus test and not be mere factoid aggregations from the web. By asking a deeper essential question which moves beyond the birth and death dates, we are asking students to synthesize the impact of an individual and make an assessment of what the world would be like had they not lived. Knowledge products can be shared with others in the form of a persuasive essay, persuasive speech, or other written or created product. Linking the person to history or science curriculum is a bonus.
Philosophy in Literature	**EQ: How does literature capture and convey ideas about the meaning of life and human ethics?** Teens are capable of abstract thought, ethical reflection, and consideration of life's big questions. Reading, writing, viewing, speaking, and listening that relates to philosophical ideas, as they are presented in literature, can be developmentally relevant and engaging. Thinking and reflecting naturally leads to consideration of opposing viewpoints and perspectives. Supporting conclusions with viable arguments and discussion of open-ended questions is certainly a part of readiness for college and the workforce as well. Short but compelling selections can spin off into short-term research and authentic debate. Careful consideration of questions that have no right or wrong answer challenges the learner to probe, make decisions, and engage peers in discussion. Shared writing can synthesize text based and original conclusions. Contemporary parallels to fictional texts can easily be found in newspapers and databases. Learners can journal about and share real-world observations of pragmatic behavior or alienation, rational selfishness or deep respect for living things, value based-decisions or situational ethics. Texts: *Siddhartha* by Herman Hesse Speeches of Native Americans in *Touch the Earth* by Edward Curtis Essays by Henry David Thoreau "A Thousand Clowns" by Herb Gardiner (motion picture and play) *Anthem or The Fountainhead* by Ayn Rand Poetry by Stephen Crane *The Jungle* by Upton Sinclair *American Tragedy* by Theodore Drieser Short stories by Franz Kafka
Hamlet and unanswerable questions	**EQ: How does critical analysis of the themes of *Hamlet* by William Shakespeare answer unanswerable questions?** Rigorous and complex Shakespearean drama has been analyzed for hundreds of years. High school English students understand that critical response to literature is a very dynamic flow of ideas. Literature that stands the test of time is visited again and again by novice and expert thinkers, and big questions elude a final and absolute answer. English students in high school and early college years are still developing their ability to deal with multiple theories or positions, any or all of which could be valid. Their brains

seek diligently for the one absolute right answer. A challenge that readies students for college and workforce thinking requires learners to read closely and evaluate critical response to *Hamlet*.

After reading the play and exploring critical essays regarding the themes of the play, students choose a theme. Using quality literary databases or print resources that provide a rich platform of critical analysis, students evaluate the strength of opposing or supporting opinion. Bloom's *Modern Critical Interpretations*, Gale's series *Shakespeare for Students*, Marjorie Garber's *Shakespeare and Modern Culture*, and Twayne's *Authors* all provide rich sources of analysis.

As the CCSS prescribes, they select the strongest and most important arguments regarding the meaning of their theme, and write an evidence-based conclusion. They share their conclusion and the process of arriving at an answer for an unanswerable question. Critical thinking made transparent or visible reinforces the learners as they use their brand new cognitive driver's license.

SOCIAL STUDIES: LESSON PLANS AND THINK TANK STARTER KITS

Country Report Alternatives: 6th Grade Social Studies, Math, and Library United Nations Summit—Proposal for International Aid

WHAT'S THE BIG IDEA?

From California to the New York Islands, country reports are being done ubiquitously. Staunchly rooted in the field guide to "Reports Everybody Loves to Hate," this report joins the ranks of bird reports, state reports, animal reports, and biography reports. Most of the time these reports merely transfer facts found on the Internet or within an encyclopedia onto paper or a PowerPoint presentation. Country reports feature factoids such as capitals, rulers, democracies, and natural resources that are reported proudly with the absolute assurance that correct answers are filling in every single box. Disaffected learners plow through the task with no hope of meaning or recall, plugging in and going to the next empty box. High flyers get out the glitter and have the thing laminated at the copy store but have no hope of recall or deep meaning.

While our students are creating "travel brochures" and filling "hypothetical suitcases," other countries are asking their students to examine *mortality rates* and brainstorm solutions for the root causes. The time has come to increase the rigor of our country reports and require kids to examine data, think, and solve real-world problems. Low-level country reports can easily be transformed into flat-world experiences by making global connections to relevant issues that even a young child can understand. By concentrating on the social studies topics of *geography, history, economy, government, culture,* and *science and technology,* students focus not on meaningless "facts" but move to cause and effect, implications of culture and geography, and more.

Brain research demonstrates that teachers can underestimate the capacity of younger students, and research says in making a lesson harder, a student's brain may be stimulated to investigate and hardwire new conceptual ideas. When the level of synthesis is reached, new knowledge becomes the building block base for future learning.

In this lesson, we are asking classroom teachers and librarians to begin with an engaging "homework hook" to mine data. This data-mining activity activates thinking and instantly breeds relevance. Students go home and investigate their pantries, refrigerators, dresser drawers, and electronic products for countries of origin. This eye-opening activity brings to light the enduring understanding of global interdependency. Students return to eagerly map dots and set themselves up for brainstorming "wonder" questions for inquiry. (If this is not possible, amass 75 such items from your home and school and use those.) From this activity, students wonder, investigate, synthesize, and express (W.I.S.E.).

After choosing a country that contributes, or fails to contribute, to the global economy, students engage in an investigation of their country and prepare to represent it as a U.N. ambassador. After students research to discover the promise and perils of their chosen nation, they will need to synthesize this information to speak intelligently as that country's ambassador.

COUNTRY REPORT MATH AND DATA FOCUS

An embedded piece of this unique United Nations Summit incorporates math, creating an interdisciplinary learning experience blending ELA, social studies, and math. Extending this lesson to access, select, use, and integrate data and statistics into an evidence-based claim connects math to the knowledge product and process in many ways.

- The CCSS addresses the use of data in evidence-based claims and arguments. Fact-based decision making starts with math. Understanding the world mathematically is a goal of the CCSS.
- Reading tabular and graphical information and statistics is also a part of the CCSS. Reading complex statistical texts in tabular form introduces comprehension and mathematical understanding.

Rich and authoritative data regarding health, education, environment, and economy is readily available on the Internet and in quality information resources in databases. Data will drive the choice of a problem in a country and a compelling choice for a persuasive essay or evidence-based claim presents itself. If malaria is the number-one cause of death; if only 12 percent girls receive an elementary education; if toxins left behind by oil drilling poison the water table; If only 50percent of the people are employed, etc.

To measure a problem, in natural and human terms, also drives decision making and conclusions. Comparative data from country to country spotlights problems needing to be solved. The world can be mapped by infant mortality, malnutrition, drought, unemployment, or trade.

Mathematical Examples

The World Health Organization (WHO) http://www.who.int/countries/en/ is a searchable and authoritative platform for data related to health. Each country has a detailed breakdown of data related to health. Data and statistics are also displayed comparatively and cumulatively regarding world health. WHO's Global Health Observatory portal provides access to data and analyses for monitoring global health. Data is displayed in a number of meaningful ways. Country profiles are comprehensive and detailed. For example, tuberculosis cases can be viewed in a table based on time, and it can be seen where cases are increasing or decreasing. Data can be displayed by income with the input of the Word Bank. Deaths from this disease and countless others are documented. Compelling problems jump off the tables. Links take readers to solutions, informing the learner of ways to solve specific problems.

The World Health Organization website offers data on many topics that students should not miss. Be sure to navigate and model accessing:

- Data repository
- World health statistics report
- Statistical reports
- Country statistics
- Map gallery

Education—The same broad access and useful information can be found for education through the World Bank Education Stats website: http://data.worldbank.org/topic/education#boxes-box-topic_cust_sec. Every number conveys global realities that even elude important decision makers. Learners can search their country and see a detailed profile of issues and problems.

Environmental data—The World Bank is an authoritative provider of tabular and graphical information about global environmental problems. Their site for this purpose is http://data.worldbank.org/topic/environment. The United Nations provides an Environmental Data Explorer at http://geodata.grid.unep.ch/. Learners provided with these links can search their country and ascertain the big picture, make relevant choices, and convey meaningful evidence using the statistics there.

Students are asked to find problems and solve them. This propels the activity to the top of Bloom's as students brainstorm possible causes and solutions of a nation's promise or peril. By the end of this lesson, learners have created an evidence-based claim and are ready to argue for funding to solve their country's real-world problem. As they plead for those in power to address their issue, they have reached the top of Bloom's and beyond.

Each ambassador should be ready and able to use the vocabulary of the discipline to spotlight how they contribute to the world economy, or why they are not able to. Knowledge products present alternative to former written reports.

Lesson:	United Nations Summit
Learning targets:	Students will examine a country to understand how strengths and weaknesses fit into a global economic picture Students will begin to understand the meaning of being "globally interdependent" Students will explain how policies are developed to address public problems (C3 Framework Social Studies Standards) Students will use credible databases to investigate answers Students will practice speaking with text-based answers
Essential questions:	How can we use a credible database to investigate answers? How are countries dependent upon each other? How do countries strengths and weaknesses affect their economy? How do the topography, geography, natural resources, and other factors such as population affect the economy of a country?
Text	*Hungry Planet: What the World Eats* by Peter Menzel and Faith D'Aluisio *Material World: A Global Family Portrait* by Peter Menzel, Charles C. Mann, and Paul Kennedy *If You Lived Here: Houses of the World* by Giles LaRoche and other books exposing different living conditions and concerns. Databases such as: KidsInfoBit <www.gale.cengage.com/**InfoBits**)> EBSCO Primary Search <http://www.ebscohost.com/us-elementary-schools/primary-search> eLibrary <http://www.elibrary.com> CultureGrams: <http://culturegrams.com/ and others suitable for grades 4–5 which will likely spotlight issues beyond surface facts such as holiday celebrations. URLs such as the U.S. Department of State and those listed here will give real-world data on problems, warnings, and other concerns. http://www.who.int/countries/en/—World health organization will list health concerns http://www.who.int/research/en/—Global health monitoring http://travel.state.gov/content/passports/english/country.html—may be a rigorous read www.cia.gov *World Factbook*—This site provides an lists issues and concerns http://data.worldbank.org/topic/education#boxes-box-topic_cust_sec. World Bank Education Stats http://data.worldbank.org/topic/environment—UN Environmental Data http://geodata.grid.unep.ch/—Environmental data
Power words	Global interdependency currency, mortality, economics, government, opportunity, education, opportunity, borders, and others that may become your local focus

Vocabulary of library discipline	Keywords, evidence, investigate, claim, source, credible, inquiry, research, report					
CCSS Goals	x	Vocabulary use	x	Solve real-world issues	x	Discuss, interpret, explain
	x	Nonfiction use	x	Research	x	Use formal English
	x	Close reading	x	Build and present knowledge	x	Rigor
	x	Evidence-based claim	x	Synthesis	x	Relevance
Rigor	This lesson uses data, information, and more to tap into a child's innate curiosity of their world. The EQ is difficult for an adult to answer and therefore will demonstrate the knowledge gained from all these activities. Low-level country reports are being done all around the nation. Most of the time these reports merely transfer facts found on the Internet or within an encyclopedia. However, this same subject matter may easily be transformed into a flat-world experience which makes global concepts relevant to even a young child.					
Relevance hook	We indeed live in a flat world—a globally interdependent world. The hook activity instantly instills relevance by asking students to record from home 15 countries of origin for clothes, food, and household goods. Students returning to school can represent that data in bar graphs as well as record frequency via colored dots on a paper world map. The paper world-map activity allows them the chance to visually see the concentration of world production and consumption. (Use different colored dots for food, clothing, and household goods.) It is likely that students will find many clothing dots are concentrated in China, Vietnam, India, and other "cheaper" locations. Food dots will likely be applied in Central America during winter months as well as many from within the United States. Household items will likely come from the United States, China, Korea, Malaysia, and other countries dominating manufacturing. Our inquiry endeavor begins with students' natural questioning ability. When "dots" are applied to the world map they visually indicate world economic activity. Inquisitive thinking should emerge as ten-year-olds automatically ask questions such as, "Why are there so many dots in China?" "Why are there so many food dots in Central and South America?" "Why do some countries have no dots?" "Why are we consuming so many items from other countries?" and so forth.					
Reader and the task	The knowledge product for this research endeavor can take many formats. Examine the following and craft your own UN focused endeavor. Here are a few knowledge products and ideas that you could discuss with classroom teachers as an alternative to former written reports: • After students research to discover the promises and perils of their chosen nation, they will need to synthesize this information to speak intelligently as that country's ambassador. Each ambassador should be ready and able to use the vocabulary of the discipline to spotlight how they contribute to the world economy, or why they are not able to. • Mock U.N. General Assembly with "ambassadors" pleading for international monetary aid to solve problems. (Evidence-based claim) Principals pose as the Head of the United Nations and award funding.					

	• Create a mock U.S. Department of State website (Smore.com, wikis, spotlights problems and recommended solutions (i.e., the evidence-k collaborative group). • Create an infographic for the nation presenting your promises and po. tions to our flat world. (Piktochart.com or paper products) • Each group can prepare a script for their U.N. address and record it via Audacity. Students can collaboratively build a *Virtual World Map* with Thinglink.com hotspots on their country. These hotspots connect to Audacity recordings of their U.N. address. If writing tasks are required as part of an ELA assessment, each student could write a persuasive argument paper building from the EBC that they constructed for their country. This could be done in the first-person voice of the ambassador or another representative that they have discovered to brainstorm their questions either in groups or collectively as a class.
Assessment	• The essential questions serve as pre- and post-assessment tools as student use the vocabulary of the discipline to articulate their conclusions. • Graphic organizer for creating an evidence-based claim. (follows) • Rubrics for presentation assessing: quality, critical thinking, and original conclusions; use of carefully selected detail; and sense of audience and purpose. • Formative assessment or planning and organizing a persuasive speech guides the process and the product. • Student self-assessment bookmarks are recommended to keep students on task and help them pace themselves. Students would use these as a guide for finishing the task as well as insuring that the expectations are met. (See below.) • Bookmarks for distribution serve to empower the students to mastery of the vocabulary of the discipline. These words may also be used to teach search narrowing: Major words and minor words—What are you looking for and what would you like to know about it? (Angola mortality; Pakistan sweatshops; etc.) • Summative assessment rubrics used for "old" country reports can be modified to reflect the depth of answers to essential questions.
Think tank spotlight	This lesson embraces the anchor standard "research to build and present knowledge" and the close reading comes during investigation. Students are given choice and a voice in the knowledge product to transfer the learning responsibility to the learner. Students are asked to find problems, and human nature naturally tries to solve problems. This propels the activity to the top of Bloom's taxonomy as students brainstorm possible causes and solutions. By the end of this lesson, learners have created an evidence-based claim and are ready to argue for funding to solve their country's real-world problem. As they plead for those in power to address their issue, they have reached the top of Bloom's taxonomy and beyond. They have experienced these thinking activities: • Inferring and reasoning • Drawing conclusions • Using thinking and not just experience • Framing possibilities as well as facts, ideas without actual objects • Developing complex thinking and view of the world • Expressing personal thoughts and views, have intense interests • Focusing on personal decision making • Imagining outcomes of actions • Calculating mathematically • Solving problems • Developing the ability to combine related items and classify them • Generalizing

Bloom's barometer	Remembering	Understanding	Applying	Analyzing	Evaluating	Creating
• Thinking creatively • Beginning to monitor and control thinking • Planning						
	X	X	X	X	X	X

Standards spotlight	**National Social Studies Standards**
	• Construct maps to represent and explain the spatial patterns of cultural and environmental characteristics.
	• Explain how the relationship between the environmental characteristics of places and production of goods influences the spatial patterns of world trade.
	• Present a summary of arguments and explanations to others outside the classroom using print and oral technologies (e.g., posters, essays, letters, debates, speeches, and reports) and digital technologies (e.g., Internet, social media, and digital documentary).
	• Critique arguments for credibility.
	• Draw on disciplinary concepts to explain the challenges people have faced and opportunities they have created, in addressing local, regional, and global problems at various times and places.
	• Evaluate alternative approaches or solutions to current economic issues in terms of benefits and costs for different groups and society as a whole.
	• Identify examples of the variety of resources (human capital, physical capital, and natural resources) that are used to produce goods and services.
	
	Common Core
	ELA
	• Use precise language and domain-specific vocabulary to inform about or explain the topic.
	• Refer to details and examples in a text when explaining what the text says explicitly and when drawing inferences from the text.
	• Draw evidence from literary or informational texts to support analysis, reflection, and research.
	• Explain events, procedures, ideas, or concepts in a historical, scientific, or technical text, including what happened and why, based on specific information in the text.
	• Interpret information presented visually, orally, or quantitatively (e.g., in charts, graphs, diagrams, time lines, animations, or interactive elements on web pages) and explain how the information contributes to an understanding of the text in which it appears.
	• Integrate information from two texts on the same topic in order to write or speak about the subject knowledgeably.
	• Draw on information from multiple print or digital sources, demonstrating the ability to locate an answer to a question quickly or to solve a problem efficiently.
	• Speaking and Listening Standards: Discuss, interpret, explain, present claims and findings, use formal English
	
	[© Copyright 2010. National Governors Association Center for Best Practices and Council of Chief State School Officers. All rights reserved.]
	
	Mathematics
	  • Represent and interpret data
	  • Reason abstractly and quantitatively
	
	[© Copyright 2010. National Governors Association Center for Best Practices and Council of Chief State School Officers. All rights reserved.]

Evidence-Based Claim: Show me the evidence!	
Claim:	
Evidence:	
Evidence:	
Evidence:	
Data:	
Conclusion based on research:	

Self-assessment Checklist

Task Accomplished	Choose a country to represent as an *Ambassador* and prepare yourself to address the United Nations
	We have read about our country.
	We can identify real-world problems for our country and explain why we consider these important.
	We have chosen a few problems to investigate.
	We are listing strengths and positive points.
	We can identify keywords for investigating our real-world problem.
	We can read about our country and find evidence from databases and approved government sites to find facts, data, and evidence for our cause.
	We have identified a significant problem or two for our country.
	I can find credible information on my team's chosen problem.
	I can assess whether my information in credible, accurate, and usable.
	I or We have built an evidence-based claim.
	I am ready to argue why this problem needs to be addressed by people in power.
	I am ready to discuss our real-world problem with the class and have used evidence to support my claim.
	We are ready to use our power words our address to the United Nations.

Power Words of Country Reports	Power Words of Country Reports	Power Words of Country Reports
Ambassador	Ambassador	Ambassador
Border	Border	Border
Capital	Capital	Capital
Consume	Consume	Consume
Continent	Continent	Continent
Country	Country	Country
Culture	Culture	Culture
Democracy	Democracy	Democracy
Economy	Economy	Economy
Employment	Employment	Employment
Equator	Equator	Equator
Geography	Geography	Geography
Government	Government	Government
Inoculations	Inoculations	Inoculations
Mortality	Mortality	Mortality
Natural resources	Natural resources	Natural resources
Produce	Produce	Produce
Topography	Topography	Topography
Travel advisory	Travel advisory	Travel advisory
United Nations	United Nations	United Nations
Others I've found:	Others I've found:	Other I've found:

News, Noise, Fights, and the Bill of Rights! Is the Bill of Rights Still Relevant?   Grades 7–8

WHAT'S THE BIG IDEA?

Social studies topics are often a natural connection to library research as students bring history to life. Middle school teachers should welcome the opportunity to wake up curriculum that tweens view as dry. The Bill of Rights is one of those topics, which without relevance would be easily forgotten—and whose relevance could not be more important in our freedom-challenged world. This lesson will connect a primary source document written over 200 years ago to the learner's world, and they will remember the content due to hands-on investigation and self-determined relevance.

Whether you collaborate with a classroom teacher spotlighting the Bill of Rights or do this lesson during your scheduled library time, you can teach CCSS-style. This lesson embraces all the shifts of the Common Core which have been carefully woven together. Your students will be able to recall items in the Bill of Rights, and you will be supporting academic achievement while teaching information literacy principles.

This lesson asks your students to investigate and connect history with current events. Using local newspapers, students should be able to connect the amendments in the Bill of Rights with breaking news. This breeds the relevance that the Common Core wants to incubate in instruction. Without relevance, material rarely moves to long-term memory.

This will provide you with an opportunity to metacognitively model. Research shows that when students who cannot think hear thinking out loud, they learn to think. This lesson asks higher-level thought questions such as: Is the Bill of Rights still relevant today? *What other countries would benefit from our Bill of Rights?* Which problem should be solved first? The identification of issues or problems from a reading to real life represents a transfer of information from abstraction to reality, and some children may find this difficult.

In this lesson young students are challenged to realize that our 200-plus-year-old Bill of Rights still is relevant and vitally important. With this understanding, they can venture out into a short-term research project to identify other countries which might benefit from our model. This may only occur at a rudimentary level, but the exercise of identifying real issues and finding solutions is a valuable one. Learners will experience thinking modeled by their peers and the collective minds of a group will produce a better solution than individually.

You can have an evidence-based discussion and debate over real-world oppressed countries who may need the Bill of Rights. This final debate or fishbowl discussion can provide opportunity to embrace speaking and listening standards also. You can build a rubric, which requires them to use those power words and research in their evidence-based claim.

Lesson:	News, Noise, Fights, and the Bill of Rights
Learning targets	• Students will understand the eternal relevance of our U.S. Constitution's Bill of Rights and amendments. • Students will research to identify problems and brainstorm action plans for change. • Problem solving, reasoning with evidence, communication of conclusions based on evidence
Essential questions Guiding questions	Is the Bill of Rights still relevant today? Would our model of government be a better choice for many societies? What other countries are currently experiencing similar issues that we have had in our past? How would our Bill of Rights fit into their countries' governance? Does their culture value individual rights?

Text	Local and national newspapers: (Newspaper Lexile ranges vary from a low of fourth-grade level to the *New York Times* whose front page averages a high school level.)
	Some newspapers such as the *New York Daily News* have a lower Lexile level, but also tend to report news depicting elements within the Bill of Rights.
	Primary source document: U.S. Constitution's Preamble and Bill of Rights
	(18 Amendments—and others if you choose)
	Databases for searching and close reading
Power words	Arise, compel, compensation, compulsory, confront, consent, construe, controversy, delegate, deny, deprived, disparage, enumerate, exceed, excessive, grievance, impartial, impose, indict, infamous, inflict, infringe, limb, probable, quartered, redress, seizure, violate
Library vocabulary	Analyze, evaluate, synthesize, inquiry, critical thinking, problem solving, keywords, reliability, authority, representation, problem solving, evidence, data, analysis

CCSS Goals	x	Vocabulary use	x	Solve real-world issues	x	Discuss, interpret, explain
	x	Nonfiction use	x	Research	x	Use formal English
	x	Close reading	x	Build and present knowledge	x	Rigor
	x	Evidence-based claim	x	Text-based answers	x	Relevance

Rigor	Standards in the CCSS have been designed for college and career readiness. Research consistently identifies rote learning and memorization as strategies that fall short of deep understanding and formative knowledge. Only when students manipulate and apply content will they gain deep understanding. This lesson strives to take typically "dry" material and bring it to life.
	The act of comparing, contrasting, and analyzing news reports from our culture to another requires synthesis of facts and scenarios. Close reading of a primary source document is rigorous in itself. When the Bill of Rights' deep meaning is layered over other news, cultures, and scenarios, students will deeply analyze.
	This lesson asks students to speak knowingly using academic vocabulary words. Communicating clearly and logically about complex and related functions is the final step.
Relevance	The lesson combines rigorous reading with real-life scenarios. Real-world current applications transfer history to today and thus support the National Social Studies goal of modeling change over time. Choice optimizes motivation.
	Texts contribute to a solution or a new idea. Sharing and modeling for peers, along with collaboration, make the project approach a relevant way to learn.

From *Think Tank Library: Brain-Based Learning Plans for New Standards, Grades 6–12* by Mary Boyd Ratzer and Paige Jaeger. Santa Barbara, CA: Libraries Unlimited. Copyright © 2015.

Reader and the task	Provided with a list of the first 18 amendments, students engaged in this lesson have an obvious purpose for reading newspapers as you ask them to find the Bill of Rights in the news. They will have to identify a problem from the past to connect to current day issues. The graffitti wall serves as a central location to share connections as articles are cut out, posted to the wall, and labeled.
	Between reading amendments and searching for modern-day examples, librarian or teacher can choose to practice academic vocabulary of the discipline by playing "quiz-quiz trade." See directions at end.
	After identifying an issue for international investigation, students can work either collaboratively or individually to plan a research strategy that will help them be successful. They will be tasked with creating an evidence-based claim.
	Librarian and teacher should model the path from problem identification to information investigation. This metacognitive model will then serve as an example for students to make other connections themselves with an issue
	Keywords and search terms may need to be brainstormed. Librarians can identify international new sources they recommend.
	Organization and planning will be needed to frame a model or representation. Readers will have to effectively navigating language, mathematical concepts, and effective communication.
Assessment	Formative:
	• Graffiti wall—Have students build a graffiti wall of the Bill of Rights with cut-our articles from the newspapers. As they identify amendments in the newspapers, they cut and label these on a bulletin board or a paper wall. Students should identify, note, and discuss vacancies.
	• Checklist for process and expectations (see example)
	Post-Assessment or Summative Ideas:
	• Hold a Bill or Rights symposium discussion. See the Bill of Rights discussion rubric for student self-assessment.
	• Write a journal narrative written from the perspective of someone with a problem that an up-coming amendment from the Bill of Rights would solve.
	• Write a journal article from the perspective of a citizen from the country researched.
	• Write an argument or persuasive writing piece for an *Amendment Watch Newspaper* spotlighting international violations of an amendment. Include evidence, citations, data, and credible reasoning.
Think tank spotlight	• Develop abstract thinking and reasoning
	• Synthesize from multiple sources
	• Connect a concept to the real-world
	• Gather, use, cite evidence
	• Distinguishing relevance, usefulness
	• Begin to reason deductively
	• Prefer active learning and peer interaction
	• Infer and reason, drawing conclusions using thinking and not just experience
	• Solve problems
	• Move new learning into long term memory when information connects with reality

Standards spotlight	**Common Core** **Reading for Information** Draw on information from multiple print or digital sources, demonstrating the ability to locate an answer to a question quickly or to solve a problem efficiently. Integrate information from several texts on the same topic in order to write or speak about the subject knowledgeably. **Writing** Use precise language and domain-specific vocabulary to inform about or explain the topic. Write informative/explanatory texts to examine a topic and convey ideas, concepts, and information through the selection, organization, and analysis of relevant content. [© Copyright 2010. National Governors Association Center for Best Practices and Council of Chief State School Officers. All rights reserved.] National Social Studies Standards encourages teachers to package content with a sharper focus on: • Purposes • Questions for exploration • Knowledge: what learners need to understand • Processes: what learners will be capable of doing • Products: how learners demonstrate understanding Please notice how these SS goals were woven into this lesson: [http://www.socialstudies.org/standards/curriculum]					
Bloom's barometer	Remembering	Understanding	Applying	Analyzing	Evaluating	Creating
	x	x	x	x	x	x

Directions for Quiz-Quiz Trade

This learning activity can be done in the classroom or library after the close reading of the U.S. Constitution's Bill of Rights. This is an example of how to actively use vocabulary words to help drive words into productive vocabulary language.

- Copy vocabulary reproducible back-to-back creating vocabulary cards (one for everyone) with a word on one side and definition on the opposite side
- Each child starts with a card and quizzes another student on the meaning. "Do you know what *quartered* means?" The partner is looking at the word and the student has to describe it using the words on the back (meaning).
- The other child then quizzes the partner on his word—perhaps uses it in a sentence, etc.
- Students trade cards and quiz someone else.
- This continues until all words have been used and traded.

Student Self-assessment–Process Guide

Task Accomplished	Task
	We can identify real-world problems in the news, and explain their connection to our Bill of Rights amendments. Label amendment connection.
	We can identify keywords for investigating our real-world amendment connection.
	We can find credible information on our team's chosen amendments-problem
	We can assess whether our information in credible, accurate, and usable
	We can create a claim: *[Which country or countries]* *would benefit from our Bill of Rights?*
	We have embedded at least five Bill of Rights academic vocabulary power words into our claim.
	We are ready to discuss our real-world problems with the class and have used evidence to support our claim.
	We ready to argue why this problem needs to be addressed by people in power and are ready to suggest solutions

Our real-world problem needing an action plan for change is:
Reason:
Evidence from a credible source:
Information from a credible source:
Data from a credible source:
Team recommendations for change or concern:
Library research time—Real-world problems

DISCUSSION AND DEBATE RUBRIC—ALIGNED WITH CCSS SPEAKING AND LISTENING STANDARDS

CRITERIA	We did this well!	GOOD TRY - a bit	We missed this
We are prepared and ready with information and evidence for a discussion.			
We made connections to what others said.			
We broadened discussion, by adding information			
We did not speak from our opinion, but spoke from our evidence (information)			
We sought to include others in our discussion (What did you mean by, I would argue that. . . please explain. . .)			
We spoke with our academic vocabulary and library vocabulary (At least 5 words)			
We enhanced other's discussion with our evidence, information (Or detected flawed logic)			
We referred to our evidence and information to back up our claim			
We used proper English and spoke confidently.			
We used multimedia, articles, or other media for a bonus.			

Amendment	Bail
Slander	Libel
Grievance	Militia
Quartered	Seizures

Sum of money for temporary release of accused awaiting trial	*Formal change to the US Constitution*
A false statement damaging a person's reputation (often written)	False *spoken* damaging statement
Military force raised up from civil population	A real or imagined wrong—cause for complaint
Action of capturing something, using force	To be lodged

Reconstruction, Civil Rights, and Grant's Moral War   Grade 11

WHAT'S THE BIG IDEA?

Through this unit, students are actively engaged in sustained research and critical thinking regarding the Reconstruction era as it relates to Ulysses S. Grant. Students will understand the key ideas of the social studies curriculum through a critical lens of select historical documents. Students will read through a continuum of primary texts beginning with early testimony regarding Grant's actions towards freedmen and runaway slaves during the Civil War.

As students move through to the Reconstruction era, students will:

- Read testimony from black leaders who attribute civil rights actions and moral motivation to Grant
- Closely read Grant's speeches
- Uncover Grant's commitment to civil rights
- Analyze constitutional amendments and laws passed during Grant's presidency
- Discuss the historical implications and the climate that generated laws
- Learn strategies to actively read and generate a broader vocabulary as they work individually and in groups.
- Participate in class discussion on issues, such as the southern mindset, civil rights, and suffrage
- Increase their critical thinking and discussion skills

Students will define and frame questions about Reconstruction, civil rights, and suffrage by constructing plausible arguments using inferences from evidence. Additionally, students will extrapolate meaningful and coherent connections from the past into the present. As the unit progresses, students will conduct sustained research and expound upon evidence-based claims in the voices of a citizen of the time addressing their representative in Congress.

Thinking and understanding is generated through discussion based on texts, multiple perspectives, civil rights issues over time, and short research initiatives. Speaking and writing to analyze big ideas and evidence-based claims critically engages the learner. Social interaction enhances the quality of thinking as learners work together to uncover the past, and deepen their understanding and perspective.

Lesson:	Reconstruction, Civil Rights, and *Grant's Moral War* *What's Up with the South?* *This is a collaborative ELA, Social Studies, Library Grade 11 Unit*
Learning Targets	**SS Content** Efforts to reunite the country through Reconstruction were contested, resisted, and had long-term consequences. The civil rights codified in new amendments to the Constitution were threatened and undermined by persistent racial segregation in the United States. Amendments to the Constitution were added to grant rights of citizenship and equality for African Americans with varying degrees of effectiveness. Conflicting political, economic, social, and sectional perspectives on Reconstruction led to resistance by many Southern individuals and states. Legislation and court decisions confined African Americans to the status of second-class citizens, denying them their constitutional rights from the Reconstruction era until the modern civil rights movement.

	Forms of racial discrimination which developed in the years following the Civil War varied by region.
	ELA content (Taken from CCSS ELA standards)
	Reading for Information
	Citing textual evidence to support inferences and claims
	Determine the meaning of phrases as they are used in the text—figurative, connotative, and technical meanings.
	Delineate and evaluate reasoning in primary source documents
	Use legal reasoning to advocate for public causes
	Writing
	Write arguments to support claims
	Conduct short as well as sustained research to answer a question or solve a problem
	Gather relevant information from multiple sources
	Narrow or broaden investigations as necessary
	Gather relevant information from authoritative sources
	Assess sources and purpose of sources
	Cite sources
	Draw evidence to support analysis
	Speaking and listening
	Initiate and participate effectively in a range of collaborative discussions
	Express yourself persuasively
	[© Copyright 2010. National Governors Association Center for Best Practices and Council of Chief State School Officers. All rights reserved.]
Essential questions	How did President Ulysses S. Grant sustain and act on moral principle in his fight for civil rights?
	How did Ulysses S. Grant secure freedom and civil rights for freed slaves using the constitution, legislation, and presidential powers?
	Does Grant deserve to be on the $50 bill?
Guiding questions	If Grant gave up, what would have happened to America? Who was on his side? Who was Grant fighting? Why was it so important to continue the fight against prejudice? What if grant had no supporters? Why did people in the South continue to fight diplomatically? Physically? How can we research to find out these questions? What were the real problems in the south? *What's up with the South?*

Text	**Main Close Reading Primary Source Documents:** Frederick Douglass—**From Slavery to Freedom: The African-American Pamphlet Collection, 1824–1909**	
	Format this with a wide-right margin enabling the student to note the gist and other active reading strategies during a close reading activity. "Read with a pencil." (Readability level measures difficult, but this is chunked for easier understanding.)	
	Bruce Frohnen, The American Nation: Primary Sources, ed. Bruce Frohnen (Indianapolis: Liberty Fund, 2008). Chapter: Enforcement Act of 1870, 1871, *and 1875,* http://oll.libertyfund.org/index.php?option=com_staticxt&staticfile=show.php%3Ftitle=2282&Itemid=27	
	Suggested use as an introduction to the research task. This has been formatted for easy chunking into sections for the suggested research task introduction jig-saw activity:	
	• Ulysses S. Grant, *Second Inaugural Address,* March 4, 1873, Yale Law School: The Avalon Project, http://avalon.law.yale.edu/19th_century/grant2.asp (Possible use during research) (Flesch Kincaid level 13)	
	• Ulysses S. Grant, *Personal Memoirs of U.S. Grant, Complete,* David Widger, 2004, Project Gutenburg (#4367),http://www.gutenberg.org/files/4367/old/orig4367-h/main.htm (Possible use during research)	
	Companion ELA nonfiction reading could include: *12 Years a Slave* by Solomon Northup	
Power words (You may wish your students to build their own vocabu-lary wall as to foster ownership.)	13th Amendment 14th Amendment 15th Amendment contraband abolitionist suffrage ratify Freedman's Bureau carpetbagger Democratic Party Republican Party Civil Rights Act	Robert E. Lee Frederick Douglasdue processdissent sharecropping scalawag Reconstruction Act of 1867 Compromise of 1877 insurrectionemancipation (And other words your students identify)
Vocabulary of library discipline	primary and secondary sources, evaluate sources of information in diverse formats, analyze , multiple perspectives, synthesize, evidence-based claim, argument, inference,	

CCSS Objectives	x	Vocabulary use	x	Solve real-world issues	x	Discuss, interpret, explain
	x	Nonfiction use	x	Research	x	Use formal English
	x	Close reading	x	Build and present knowledge	x	Rigor
	x	Evidence-based claim	x	Building knowledge in the content areas	x	Relevance

Rigor	Thinking in the discipline of social studies requires the critical analysis of the existing records of the past. Often characterized by the bias of the observer, testimony regarding events, and issue presents many versions of what actually happened and why. Eleventh graders still seek to find the single authoritative voice that has the ultimate answer to the historical or issue based question. Challenging learners and supporting them at the same time with sound pedagogy, teachers can launch a quest for deep understanding through close reading of rigorous primary secondary texts. Vocabulary development and background knowledge contribute to fluency in reading complex historical texts. Discussion and analysis makes thinking transparent. Verifiable assumptions and misconceptions, stronger and weaker arguments, and defensible and specious conclusions can be interrogated and refined. Supporting claims with evidence demands higher level thought, genuine synthesis, diligent evaluation of information sources, and a departure from "I think. . ." as the only point of reference. This level of rigor can be called strategic thinking. Extended thinking would be a level higher. Extended prior knowledge, investment of work and time, planning, and application of new knowledge to the real-world characterize extended thinking. The motivated and confident learner, with strong content mastery, could achieve this, and demonstrate expert thinking in a debate, mock trial, or forum. That should be the goal.
Relevance	U. S. Grant fought a moral war for civil rights during and after the Civil War. His own words and the words of witnesses at the time provide ample testimony to this. His moral education motivated him to use administrative, legislative, and executive actions to establish civil rights in the Deep South during Reconstruction. Events and conditions in the south that warranted Grant's diligence proved to be intransigent, becoming magnified and entrenched for nearly 100 years after the Civil Rights Act of 1875. If Grant gave up, the war would have been fought in vain. Relevance and connections over time are self-evident. The civil rights movement, the Civil Rights Act of 1964, and enduring issues in America today with racism and inequality all tie the present with the past. To what degree is the present similar to the past? How do day-to-day experiences in schools, neighborhoods, and communities prove the relevance of this learning experience, and demonstrate the real-world connections for students and teachers.
Reader and the task	I can research a topic that answers a question or solves a problem. I can narrow or broaden a topic when needed. I can synthesize information from several sources on a subject. I can use evidence from many sources to support analysis, reflection, and conclusions. I can actively prepare for discussions through researching material beforehand. I can refer to texts for evidence while discussing a topic or issue. I can analyze the merits of sources based upon the task, purpose, and audience. I can maintain the flow of ideas when incorporating information into my writing. I can establish clear goals and deadlines. I can pose questions that probe reasoning and evidence. I can ensure that a broad range of positions on a topic are discussed. I can clarify, verify, or challenge ideas and conclusions. I can delineate distinctive perspectives on a subject in writing and discussions. I can incorporate different perspectives in writing and discussions.

	I can resolve contradictions and gaps in information and discussions. I can determine what more information is required to further the discussion.	
Assessment	**Pre-assessment activity: What do you know about Reconstruction?**	Mind map (Save for post-assessment comparison—or continue to mind-map throughout the unit)
	Background building Vocabulary introduction	Group discussion
	Close reading Frederick Douglass Pamphlet 1871	Discussion with text-dependent questions, graphic organizers, participation
	Close reading Contraband camps	Graphic organizers, participation in evidence-based discussion
	Evidence building practice—Enforcement Acts—Jigsaw close reading activity with groups getting a few paragraphs to identify the main idea (i.e., problem) stated.	Graphic organizers completed Smartboard, Padlet, or graffitti wall bulletin board to post "Problems Identified."
	Evidence building practice—Grant's Second Inaugural address	Evidence-based discussion, graphic organizers, self-assessment discussion/debate rubric
	Short Research: What's Up with the South? What events precipitated the Enforcement Acts? Jig-saw the Enforcement Acts: What were the cultural issues present around America that needed attention? Students will: • independently choose a civil rights issue addressed in the Enforcement Acts. • research this issue and state, within the time period of Reconstruction. • Form a knowledge product (evidence-based speech as a congressman, or letter to their congressman from the historical perspective.)	Notes, citations, sources, organized information to synthesize "Letter to their state representative" (1870s) stating why governmental action is needed to solve a problem. Students embrace vocabulary of the discipline and synthesize found facts (evidence) into original conclusions
	Historical Concept Map Connections of events and law during Reconstruction	Graphic organizer included
	Evidence-Based Presentation of "Congressional Speeches" or letters to Congressman	Rubric(s) for speaking contribution as well as rubric for an evidence-based writing assignment

Think tank spotlight	• Know that problems can be analyzed and solved • Synthesize multiple complex texts to construct big ideas and conclusions • Draw conclusions from multiple quality-information texts • Develop knowledge by testing existing beliefs against new knowledge • Reach understandings that revise or dismiss existing beliefs • Use evidence to review beliefs and understandings; debate • Identify the sources of their beliefs • Practice scientific thinking by investigating and analyzing evidence • Question the validity of inferences • Validate thinking with reason • Consider possibilities and generate alternatives • Reason and investigate to construct arguments • Can learn to reconcile opposing views when experts disagree • Progress beyond the standard of absolute certainty • Develop knowledge based on evaluation and argument					
Bloom's barometer	Remembering	Understanding	Applying	Analyzing	Evaluating	Creating
	x	x	x	x	x	x

Student self-assessment checklist:

Check off as you research, or note a question...	
	I can research a topic that answers a question or solves a problem.
	I can narrow or broaden a topic when needed.
	I can synthesize information from several sources on a subject.
	I can use evidence from many sources to support analysis, reflection, and conclusions.
	I can actively prepare for discussions through researching material beforehand.
	I can refer to texts for evidence while discussing a topic or issue
	I can analyze the merits of sources based upon the task, purpose, and audience.
	I can maintain the flow of ideas by incorporating select information into a piece of writing. I can establish clear goals and deadlines.
	I can pose questions that probe reasoning and evidence.
	I can ensure that a broad range of positions on a topic are discussed.
	I can clarify, verify, or challenge ideas and conclusions.
	I can delineate distinctive perspectives on a subject in writing and discussions.
	I can incorporate different perspectives in writing and discussions.
	I can resolve contradictions and gaps in information and discussions.
	I can determine what more information is required to further the discussion.

OPINION OR FACT: YOU BE THE JUDGE

Can you tell the difference between fact and opinion? Facts should be able to be proven, while opinion holds a value judgment that is subjective. Writers will often blur these two together to strengthen their voice. You must read like a detective.

Fact: Cigarettes have been proven to cause lung cancer.
Opinion: Smoking should be prohibited.

Factual text quotes:	
Quote	Why I knew this was fact:

Opinion text quote:	
Quote	Why I knew this was opinion:

Drawing Conclusions

Evidence I found:

Meaning I deduced:

Conclusions I've drawn:

STARTER KITS FOR SOCIAL STUDIES

Time to Launch Lessons for Your Brain Friendly Library!

Additional ideas are listed below to inspire you to build your own Inquiry-based learning endeavor with your teachers. Having read this book, you are likely equipped to develop deep student-centered learning endeavors from the ideas below.

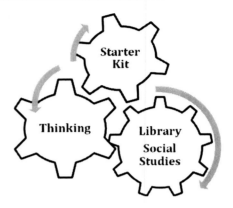

Text or content	Inquiry Lesson in Social Studies
1800s movers and shakers	EQ: If your mover or shaker were alive today, what would their vanity plate read? EQ: If your mover or shaker were alive today, what would their resume look like? Research a mover, shaker, or suffragette of your choice and be able to summarize what they stood for via a vanity plate. Visit the state's department of motor vehicles and try to create one that is not taken. Students should snapshot the vanity plate and print it. Vanity plates will be displayed on the wall where others can try to guess who's driving that car. Students will prepare a resume for their mover or shaker and be prepared to interview for jobs. Community members, parents, administrators, and others can be included in the job fair where the students will interview for jobs personifying their mover or shaker, and they should be able to speak knowledgably about their strengths and weaknesses and which jobs they would be likely to apply for. This lesson was cooperatively planned with David Brown, Saratoga Springs High School, New York.
Explorer's expertise electronically	We know that explorers set sail for the 3 Gs: Gold, Glory, and God. EQ: What was the journey like? How did their discoveries impact the world? EQ: If your explorer had access to our modern-day technology, what would their blog look like? Create a blog for your explorer. Via blog posting, create a sailing journal for the travel plans, sail, discoveries, difficulties, inspirations, observations, and impact the explorer had on the world. (If possible, try to find the primary source documents of your explorer's captain's log.) The typical seventh-grade Explorer Report can receive this twenty-first century learning makeover.
Middle Ages connection	EQ: If you were living in the Middle Ages under laws of chivalry how would your behavior have to change? Create an etiquette guide for the Middle Ages. Post this on wood (cardboard), stone, or a Smore.com post that is made to look old fashioned. To answer this question, students will have to complete a short-term research assignment. This is a good connection to the sixth-grade curriculum which often covers ancient and medieval history. Brainstormed by Salem Central Schools Librarian, Karen Fronhofer.

Ellis Island reenactment	EQ: How did individual immigrants face and sometimes overcome daunting challenges leaving their homeland to seek the American Dream? John Dewey provides the rationale for this lesson: learn by experience. Eighth graders explored the Ellis Island experience from a number of perspectives. Using Library of Congress photographs of Ellis Island, learners inductively drew conclusions about what happened there as the world's poor funneled through, yearning for freedom and opportunity. Getting inside the experience, learners took on a specific role of an immigrant, with a range of personal attributes. Age, education, work experience, skills, language barriers, health, country of origin, reasons for immigrating, children, spouses, and travel became part of many profiles for an Ellis Island reenactment. Members of the community and volunteers staged a mock Ellis Island review for each student in character. At a series of stations, students were questioned and examined in regard to their potential to be admitted to the United States or sent back to the place they left. In conversation learners were accountable for the history of their character. If they were admitted, student proceeded to an Oath of Allegiance. If not, they were prepared for deportation. *C3 Framework for Social Studies State Standards:* • Explain how cultural patterns and economic decisions influence environments and the daily lives of people in both nearby and distant places. • Classify series of historical events and developments as examples of change and/or continuity. • Evaluate how historical events and developments were shaped by unique circumstances of time and place as well as broader historical contexts. This originated at Hudson Falls Middle School, Hudson Falls, New York, with school librarian Marcia Krantz and the eighth-grade teachers. Hudson Falls Middle School also used reenactments for U.S. History in relation to westward expansion, assembly lines, Rosa Parks, and cattle drives.
Path to victory or defeat	EQ: How do events, individuals, geography, and unexpected circumstances determine the path to victory or defeat in a 20th Century War fought by the United States? Grade 11 students, toward the end of a course in U.S. History and Government, synthesize historical sources to draw conclusions about strategies, turning points, events, individuals, and the progress of 20th century American wars and conflicts. Beginning with rationale for a specific conflict, students track the path to victory or the path to defeat with a board game. Playing pieces can be people, leaders, opposing armies, military hardware, or anything else that serves the purpose of accounting for progress or setbacks in war. Students need to categorize details into big ideas of how victory was achieved or not achieved. Considerations of economics, politics, geography, home front attitudes and roles, tactical strategies, weather, weapons, and leadership could be translated into game cards or opportunities to advance or move back. The big picture emerges as learners present their path to victory/defeat products. A creative approach was frequently in evidence. This lesson was originally taught by U.S. History and Government teacher Kathy Mayba at Shenendehowa High School, Clifton Park, New York.
Revolutions	EQ: How do social, political, geographical, and historical forces converge to spark revolution? EQ: Why do people die for ideas?

	Deep understanding of the big idea of revolution is accomplished by researching and analyzing many revolutions through history. The emerging common ground of revolutions generates a conceptual grasp of this potent change agent. The specifics that distinguish one revolution from another can provide significant point of contrast, and connect an event to time and place.
	A text, Carl Sandberg's poem "Threes" introduces the unit, as it focuses on the three-word epithets that drove famous revolutions, like "Bread, peace, land" or "Liberty, Equality, Fraternity." Sandberg asks the question: why do people die for ideas?
	C3 Framework for Social Studies State Standards: • Analyze connections among events and developments in broader historical contexts. • Classify series of historical events and developments as examples of change and/or continuity. • Evaluate how historical events and developments were shaped by unique circumstances of time and place as well as broader historical contexts. • Distinguish between long-term causes and triggering events in developing a historical argument. • Generate questions about individuals and groups who have shaped significant historical changes and continuities.
Dark Ages	EQ: Why is the history of the world a history of recurring Dark Ages? EQ: Why is our time in history a Dark Age or not a Dark Age?
	Insight to the essential historic records of the nominal Dark Ages prompts the realization that there have been many Dark Ages through time in many places on the globe.
	Students in Global Studies can research historic eras where adversity pushed progress to a standstill and human suffering forward. Thoughtful analysis of the reasons for Dark Ages can be applied to contemporary events. An evidence-based argument would document a time, place, and events over time as a Dark Age in history.
	C3 Framework for Social Studies State Standards • Analyze connections among events and developments in broader historical contexts • Classify series of historical events and developments as examples of change and/or continuity • Evaluate how historical events and developments were shaped by unique circumstances of time and place as well as broader historical contexts • Distinguish between long-term causes and triggering events in developing a historical argument • Generate questions about individuals and groups who have shaped significant historical changes and continuities
Witch hunts	EQ: How do witch hunts extend beyond the historically documented events of the Middle Ages, Salem, and 15th century France to parallel occurrences in recent history?
	Scapegoating, hate crimes, oppression of minorities, and patterns of recent historical events can be researched to generate an evidence-based claim. Students synthesize primary and secondary resources to uncover a witch hunt that correlates with related historic events.
	C3 Framework for Social Studies State Standards • Analyze connections among events and developments in broader historical contexts • Organize applicable evidence into a coherent argument about the past
	Brainstormed and field-tested by Sarah McCann, Hudson Falls Middle School Librarian

World Food Program Hunger Map	EQ: How does the World Food Program Hunger Map and the date behind it present evidence that require immediate global action? EQ: Why can the world be divided into haves and have-nots? http://documents.wfp.org/stellent/groups/public/documents/communications/wfp260272.pdf Using the World Food Program Hunger Map to analyze and draw conclusions about the data displayed graphically there, students research one area of the world with a high ratio of hunger to determine causes. Students create anevidence-based claim in a media format for action from the global community. *C3 Framework for Social Studies State Standards* Economics: Evaluate alternative approaches or solutions to current economic issues in terms of benefits and costs for different groups and society as a whole. Analyze the ways in which cultural and environmental characteristics vary among various regions of the world.
The 5 Minute Advocate	EQ: How can we change the world by advocating for something we believe in just five minutes a week? Modeling her strong commitment to libraries, the school librarian works with students in government class to give them firsthand experience with advocacy. Actually visiting state legislators, the school librarian and selected students shared persuasive advocacy letters and talking points in face-to-face meetings. Seniors chose a real-world problem or issue that fell under state government, and generated evidence-based arguments for legislative action. An authentic product and process brought the world to school and gave a sense of personal voice making a difference to each student. *C3 Framework for Social Studies State Standards* • Analyze how people use and challenge local, state, national, and international on a variety of public issues. • Apply a range of deliberative and democratic strategies and procedures to make decision and take action in their classrooms, schools, and out-of-school civic contexts. This unit idea originated with Amy Carpenter, school librarian at Stillwater Junior Senior High School, Stillwater, New York.
World religions	**EQ: In a religion of the world, what defines the good man?** Using primary texts and secondary information resources, construct an evidence-based claim about what makes a good man in a specific world religion. Analyze what cultural or historic forces resulted in that ethical perspective. Compare and contrast the religions of the world from this core religious concept.
Westward expansion	**EQ: How would those who were a part of westward expansion in America reflect on their role and their actions in a conversation with contemporaries about change for the better and change for the worse?** Taking on the roles of key players in the westward expansion of the United States, learners research the history of that era. Using primary and secondary sources, learners synthesize speeches, letters, and texts by recreating the beliefs, motivations, purpose, and actions of a representative figure in conversation with an historical contemporary.

	Paying close attention to the perspective that the historical documents take, learners see history through a lens that needs to be understood and analyzed.

With the role players addressing issues, problems, decisions, and actions, they debate in character whether this time of change was for the better or the worse. |
| **Civilizations** | **EQ: What are the essential cultural, economic, educational, social, political, and technological attributes of a civilization?**

Inductively analyze the early civilizations in world history, concluding the ways in which they can be distinguished as civilizations. Using a formula for "What makes a civilization," learners create a civilization with geographic, economic, political, technological, social, cultural and historic features, in effect presenting evidence that their composite is a civilization. |
| **Wall of the wealthy** | **EQ: How do the super-wealthy use their money to change the world—either intentionally or unintentionally?**
EQ: Is money power?

Throughout history wealthy individuals have acquired, amassed, hoarded, and shared their wealth. They have impacted cultures for the good and bad. From Robert Morris who financed the American Revolution to Bill Gates who is trying to eradicate malaria, we have seen that money is power. This investigation will ask students to examine the cause and effect of how wealthy movers and shakers have changed the world—for good or bad.

Students should be given a list of possibilities or be allowed to choose a differing individual they may identify. Students will create an evidence-based claim for the impact their person had on history.

In a court of public opinion, students will share their philanthropist or ultra-wealthy individual, and a class ruling for good, bad, and ugly can be rendered.

Place face-profiles on a timeline and have a discussion related to global history.

C3 Framework for Social Studies State Standards:
• Analyze connections among events and developments in broader historical contexts
• Organize applicable evidence into a coherent argument about the past |

Economics—Senior Five-Year Plan: Are You in the Black?
Think Critically and Advocate Persuasively

WHAT'S THE BIG IDEA?

Jason Groak, a high school economics teacher in Salem, New York, knew his students had delusions of grandeur, and he cooked up this lesson to give them a dose of reality. As high school seniors plan for the future, they dreams of their own apartments, new cars, and independence. These dreams are not reasonable for graduates who plan to go right to work after high school at minimum wage.

Hopes and dreams do not transfer to real life without planning and hard work. Many high school seniors are making decisions that determine their economic futures with a good measure of half-truths, misconceptions, hopes, dreams, conventional wisdom, and guesswork. Those considering dropping out of school could have a shocking wake-up call when they look closely at the real-world through the lens of a budget, employment statistics, education levels, and projected income. Four years of college degrees will likely cost a graduate $30,000 of debt, and this is awaiting graduates as they walk across the stage with their diploma. Starting salaries and college loans can mean untenable financial stress, and Economics class may be the place to think this through.

Data-driven decision making is extremely relevant for teenagers who dream big and underestimate costs. This lesson applies the economics of:

○ cost of living,

○ projected earnings,

○ budgeting,

○ loan payback schedules,

○ interest rates on loans, and

○ inflation.

Seniors analyze their own personal fiscal sustainability and risks. Thoughtfully reading statistical resources like the *Occupational Outlook Handbook* and *Statistical Abstract of the United States*, seniors document employment prospects in their chosen field, economic predictors for specific job clusters, and cost of living trends. Credit ratings, credit cards, and living within the limits of income get a close and thoughtful look. Beyond that, they become aware of the consequences of making bad choices.

Seniors interview a panel of returning graduates who have been in school or work for a year or two. They interview a local banker and a college financial aid officer who visit their class by Skype. Questions are thoughtfully developed beforehand.

Despite the best efforts of counselors, parents, and teachers the cold, hard facts can be elusive. As a portal into fact-based decision making, this lesson has the school librarian and the teacher breaking a trail for informed process and critical thinking. The initial spreadsheet is the starting point. Using Excel spreadsheets, Economics students generate a five-year plan. They complete accurate cost analysis and price out their anticipated lifestyle. Beginning with their ideal, they compare costs versus earnings. Students revise their plan as research fills in a picture of the challenges and problems that present themselves.

Meaningful discussion leads to questions and the identification of problems to be solved. Research questions are developed. Researching the current status of minimum wage legislation, college loans, and other identified issues, students make evidence-based claims.

Students brainstorm solutions, and interest rates usually top the list of targets for advocacy.

Equipping themselves with well-founded arguments, students write a persuasive letter to their legislative representatives. Just as they become old enough to vote, they communicate with their evidence-based claim supporting legislative action.

Lesson:	**Economics—Senior Five-Year Plan: Are You in the Black?** **Cost Analysis and Legislative Advocacy**
Learning Targets:	• Students generate and analyze personal economic data • Students create a five-year financial plan leveraging costs against income • Students generate questions and use information to answer them • Students verify economic projections using authoritative statistical information • Students identify gaps and contradictions in their thinking, and verify the strengths and weaknesses of their five-year financial plans • Students draw conclusions using data, and identify problems that need to be solved in their five year plan • Students read quality information sources to build background knowledge, and refine research questions, preliminary to an evidence-based claim that connects an economic problem/solution for them with legislative action through advocacy • Students synthesize multiple statistical and policy information sources, and write an evidence-based argument expressed in a letter to a legislator
Essential questions:	Are you in the black? What's your bottom line going to be? How can we advocate for what we believe is right?
Text	*Occupational Outlook Handbook 2014–2015* *Statistical Abstracts of the United States* *Pathways to Success: Integrating Learning with Life and Work to Increase National College Completion*, A Report to Congress, 2012, Advisory Committee on Student Financial Assistance http://www2.ed.gov/about/bdscomm/list/acsfa/ptsreport2.pdf Consumer Price Index by the Bureau of Labor Statistics http://www.bls.gov/cpi/ Economic and Employment Projection 2012–2022 by the Bureau of Labor Statistics http://www.bls.gov/news.release/ecopro.toc.htm Occupations with the largest projected number of job openings due to growth and replacement needs, 2012 and projected 2022 http://www.bls.gov/news.release/ecopro.t08.htm Federal Student Aid, Department of Education https://studentaid.ed.gov/
Power words	Economic trends, projections, data, statistical, employment, trends, cost analysis, income, cost of living, FAFSA, default, student debt, policy, legislation, minimum wage, Pell Grants, financial aid, predictors, projections, cost of living, Bureau of Labors Statistics, Department of Education, inflation, education level, projected earnings, credit rating
Vocabulary of library discipline	Questions, assumptions, misconceptions, verify, validate, evaluate, analyze, synthesize, conclusions, justify, evidence-based, argument, Excel, expert opinion, data, analysis, Skype, critical thinking, advocacy

CCSS shifts	x	Vocabulary use	x	Solve real-world issues	x	Discuss, interpret, explain
	x	Nonfiction use	x	Research	x	Use formal English
	x	Close reading	x	Build and present knowledge	x	Rigor
	x	Evidence-based claim	x	Text-based answers	x	Relevance

Rigor	• Looking critically at the thinking that went into their dreams and plans, students reflect on the need for solid data and evidence. • Pursuing data and statistics in often very rigorous. The brain might prefer to avoid the fine lined detail, and the overload of projections. With guidance, modeling, and support, seniors can achieve a revised five-year plan that is realistic and verifiable. • Synthesizing evidence for a persuasive letter to a legislator demands the highest levels of thinking, and long-term formative knowledge on many economic fronts.
Relevance	As Millennials would say, "this is a no-brainer." Relevance is omnipresent in every step of this lesson. The process begins with and ends with the individual. Choice, voice, problem solving, real-life payoff, and ultimate cognitive growth are immediate, personal, real, and so appropriate to seniors studying economics.
Reader and the task	Students gather and analyze data to make and revise decisions. Students determine patterns and present data to support a conclusion. Students research a topic that answers a question or solves a problem. Students evaluate information sources. Students synthesize evidence from many sources to support conclusions. Students pose questions that probe reasoning behind decisions. Students draw valid conclusions from texts. Students evaluate evidence used for arguments. Students clarify, verify, or challenge ideas and conclusions. Students resolve contradictions and gaps in information. Students organize the most important evidence to support an argument. Students use texts and data to write an evidence-based argument.
Assessment	Summative: Students will create a spreadsheet showing the costs of their goals and dreams. A bottom line supported with evidence and citations sums up their learning. Persuasive letters written to legislators are graded.
Think-tank spotlight	• Plan long term and use thinking to make life decisions • Use thinking strategies and modify them • Know that problems can be analyzed and solved • Synthesize multiple complex texts to construct big ideas and conclusions • Draw conclusions from multiple quality-information texts

	• Develop knowledge by testing existing beliefs against new knowledge • Grow in confidence as a thinker, understanding personal strengths or weaknesses • Grow in self-awareness, potential possibilities • Grow in information processing skills • Grow in core knowledge related to many disciplines • Question more consistently; question with a purpose • Solve problems better with a social group • Use distributed intelligence effectively with multiple minds in a social setting • Reach understandings that revise or dismiss existing beliefs • Identify the sources of their beliefs • Validate thinking with reason • Consider possibilities and generate alternatives Reason and investigate to construct arguments
Standards spotlight	**C3 National Social Studies Standards** • Explain how supporting questions contribute to an inquiry and how, through engaging source work, new compelling and supporting questions emerge. • Determine the kinds of sources that will be helpful in answering compelling and supporting questions, taking into consideration multiple points of view represented in the sources, the types of sources available, and the potential uses of the sources. • Analyze how people use and challenge local, state, national, and international laws to address a variety of public issues. • Analyze how incentives influence choices that may result in policies with a range of costs and benefits for different groups. • Use marginal benefits and marginal costs to construct an argument for or against an approach or solution to an economic issue. **Common Core Standards** • Integrate and evaluate multiple sources of information presented in diverse formats and media (e.g., visually, quantitatively, as well as in words) in order to address a question or solve a problem • Write arguments focused on *discipline-specific content.* • Develop claim(s) and counterclaims fairly and thoroughly, supplying the most relevant data and evidence for each while pointing out the strengths and limitations of both claim (s) and counterclaims in a discipline-appropriate form that anticipates the audience's knowledge level, concerns, values, and possible biases. [© Copyright 2010. National Governors Association Center for Best Practices and Council of Chief State School Officers. All rights reserved.]

Bloom's barometer	Remembering	Understanding	Applying	Analyzing	Evaluating	Creating
	X	X	X	X	X	X

STARTER KITS FOR ECONOMICS/BUSINESS

Text or Content	Inquiry Lesson in Economics/Business
Does social responsibility sell?	**EQ: Why does social responsibility sell?** Students in Business Communications use quality research resources, print and digital, to determine whether or not companies that use social responsibility in their advertising or corporate brand succeed in selling their products. Students share their data-based conclusions using presentation programs like Prezi, effectively communicating their analysis with original conclusions and pertinent detail. Success of advertising campaigns and corporate branding that features social responsibility is documented with data. A composite of sales trends associated with responsible production and conscientious marketing is an infographic knowledge product collaboratively constructed. An authentic process involves reaching out to local corporate and business interests who are interviewed and questioned regarding the topic. This assists students in developing their research question and planning their investigation. *C3 Framework for Social Studies State Standards* • Analyze the ways in which incentives influence what is produced and distributed in a market. • Explain how economic decisions affect the well-being of individuals, businesses, and society. • Describe the consequences of competition in specific markets. This lesson originated in the Heatly School, Green Island Union Free School District, Green Island, New York, with Business Communications teacher Marilyn Michaels and school librarian Donna Eager
Distribution of wealth	**EQ: Should America be a nation of very rich, very poor, and a dwindling middle class due to the distribution of wealth?** Texts: *Gospel of Wealth* by Andrew Carnegie "The Richest of the Rich, Proud of a New Gilded Age" by Louis Uchitelle, *New York Times,* July 15, 2007 "Why We Are in a New Gilded Age" by Paul Krugman, *New York Times Review of Books,* May 8, 2014 *Statistical Abstract of the U.S.* Learners in teams investigate and document the distribution of wealth in America with data. They then represent it graphically from 1950 to the present. Selected anecdotal facts, comparisons, and trends are also used to analyze shifts in wealth distribution since 1950. Each team is responsible for sharing significant information. Learners develop questions for inquiry, using the aggregate of documentation. Making a choice of a relevant area to research, teams construct an evidence-based argument regarding the impact of an economy of very rich and very poor. They propose strategies to remedy impacts. In an economic summit with local legislators, students share their arguments, question the arguments of others, and engage critically to draw up a prioritized action plan to address this trend locally and beyond.

	C3 Framework for Social Studies State Standards • Use economic indicators to analyze the current and future state of the economy • Use appropriate data to evaluate the state of employment, unemployment, inflation, total production, income, and growth in the economy
Corporate codes of conduct	**EQ: How do codes of conduct for corporations, colleges, military branches, and employers guide the choices of students as they transition to life after high school?** Students build background knowledge of codes or conduct and codes of ethics in a variety of real-world contexts. These include work places, higher education, and the military. Organizations that oversee professions and public service institutions could also be included. Web access to this type of information is readily available as students investigate ethics in a relevant business setting, job, college or other post-secondary setting. In a real-world analysis of the codes, students interview local employers, college deans, local citizens belong to professions, and other relevant community members. They explore and uncover in databases and newspapers consequences of breeching these codes. Organizing and synthesizing what they have learned, students in teams generate a publication intended for teens that informs them of the ethical considerations of life after high school. A real-world audience will reflect and think about these publications, when they are effectively written and designed. This lesson originated in the Heatly School, Green Island Union Free School District, Green Island, New York, with Business Communications teacher Marilyn Michaels and school librarian Donna Eager.

STEM (Science and Math): Lesson Plans and Think Tank Starter Kits

SLOPE AND THE REAL-WORLD: MAKING DECISIONS WITH MATH

The Big Idea: Secondary Mathematics, Algebra

A key idea of the CCSS in Mathematics is deep understanding sufficient to see the world mathematically and use math to make real-world decisions. Real-world connections can offset the "Why do we have to do this?" moments. Slope is a rich choice for real-world math, since it is inevitably everywhere and affects many day-to-day experiences. Choices and decisions based on slope abound. Authentic problem-solving melds math and inquiry. Formulas make sense. Observation and analysis transforms the algebra of slope into practical, important, and even fun encounters.

- I want to go hiking next week. This trail is 2 miles long and goes up 1,500 feet in altitude. This other trail is 3 miles long and goes up 500 feet. What trail will I hike?
- I have to build a ramp for handicap access to my business. How steep should it be to be convenient for users? Is there a building code for ramps?
- I saw Niagara Falls last summer, and the river was rushing so fast to the falls. Was that river going down a slope?
- Why do firefighters need to calculate slope?
- Driving in the mountains the roads have these switch backs. What's up with that?
- If I am at the gym and walk on the treadmill flat, I only burn 200 calories in 30 minutes at my usual rate. If I walk at an 11 percent incline, I burn double the calories. Why is that?
- My friend wiped out skiing this weekend. He got onto an expert trail that was so steep he lost control.
- I run on my country road. It is not flat. My left knee is always lower than my right when I run on the shoulder. What's up?
- Bike races and running races with hills demand a lot of training.
- Why does the snow slide of my neighbor's roof and not off mine?
- From the top of Pike's Peak I could see the slope of the planet in the far distance.
- Why can I only see about 10 miles out to the horizon at the beach?

Interesting stuff. Mastering a mathematical formula for calculating slope, and applying that formula in practice exercises equips a learner at only one level. Higher-level thought is required to use that mathematical knowledge to solve a problem or make a decision. The brain seeks the easy path and might be making shortcut decisions about slope all the time. "Let's not take our bikes up that way. The hills are too hard." Explaining the why and how of a decision based on mathematical principles demands deep understanding. Evidence to support a decision can be synthesized by using, manipulating, and applying the otherwise inert formula. Discussing the real-world connections with teachers and peers, students can make a choice of a real-world slope to investigate. Bringing the math to the mathematical decision, learners think critically about authentic problems. They use models and communicate. The application, analysis, and investigation of a formula deepens understanding and increases the likelihood of formative knowledge. Countries that surpass the United States in math performance target thinking and understanding of formulas instead of practice and repetition of steps.

Lesson:	Slope and the Real-World: Making Decisions with Math Secondary Mathematics, Algebra
Learning Targets	Students can apply the mathematics they know to solve problems arising in everyday life, society, and the workplace. Students use linear equations to represent, analyze, and solve a variety of problems. Students understand that the constant of proportionality (m) is the slope. They understand that the slope (m) of a line is a constant rate of change, which is observable in the real-world. Interpreting a model requires students to express a relationship between the two quantities in question. Problem solving, reasoning and proof, communication, representation, and connections (NCTM). Students use concrete objects or pictures to help conceptualize and solve a problem. They are able to identify important quantities in a practical situation and map their relationships using tools. Students investigate the mathematics of slope as it applies to a real-world problem or decision, using nonfiction information resources. Students justify a real-world decision based on slope modeling the problem, and presenting the solution in mathematical terms.
EQs	How can the math of slope contribute to real-world, informed decision making? How does the mathematics of slope impact real-world problem solving?

Text images	Topical nonfiction books connecting math and the real-world such as:
	• *The Math Dude's Quick and Dirty Guide to Algebra* by Jason Marsha
	• *Math to Build On: A Book for Those Who Build* by Johnny Hamilton
	• *Real-life Math: Everyday Use of Mathematical Concepts* by Evan Glazer
	
	Internet sources selected for reliability and authority such as:
	
	"The Physics of the Inclined Treadmill"
	http://scienceblogs.com/startswithabang/2010/03/10/the-physics-of-an-inclined-tre/
	
	"Handicap Ramp Design and Construction Guidelines"
	http://www.rcrv.org/WRAP/rampguidelines.pdf
	
	"ADA Standards for Accessible Design"
	http://www.ada.gov/2010ADAstandards_index.htm
	
	"Firefighter Math, Vertical, Horizontal, and Slope" http://www.firefightermath.org/
	U.S. Department of Transportation. Federal Highway Administration.
	    "Designing Sidewalks and Trails for Access."
	    "Clear Zones and Roadside Terrain"
	    Maintenance of Drainage Features—Slopes
	    http://safety.fhwa.dot.gov/
	Bike Trails and Slope
	http://www.trailstobuild.com/Articles/BC%20Trail%20Standards/4-3.htm
	http://www.sportsci.org/jour/9804/dps.html

Power words	Slope, y intercept, constant, proportion, formula , linear equation, grade, gradient, slope intercept form, vertical drop, elevation, angle, drainage, angle, horizontal change, vertical change, METS, two-dimensional plane

 From *Think Tank Library: Brain-Based Learning Plans for New Standards, Grades 6–12* by Mary Boyd Ratzer and Paige Jaeger. Santa Barbara, CA: Libraries Unlimited. Copyright © 2015.

Library vocabulary	Analyze, evaluate, synthesize, inquiry, critical thinking, problem solving, keywords, reliability, authority, graphical information, modeling, representation, problem solving, evidence, data, analysis
Standards spotlight	**Common Core** **Reading for Information** Draw on information from multiple print or digital sources, demonstrating the ability to locate an answer to a question quickly or to solve a problem efficiently. Integrate information from several texts on the same topic in order to write or speak about the subject knowledgeably. **Writing** Use precise language and domain-specific vocabulary to inform about or explain the topic. Write informative/explanatory texts to examine a topic and convey ideas, concepts, and information through the selection, organization, and analysis of relevant content. **Mathematics** Understand the connections between proportional relationships, lines, and linear equations. Graph proportional relationships, interpreting the unit rate as the slope of the graph. Compare two different proportional relationships represented in different ways. For example, compare a distance–time graph to a distance–time equation to determine which of two moving objects has greater speed. See corestandards.org [© Copyright 2010. National Governors Association Center for Best Practices and Council of Chief State School Officers. All rights reserved.]

CCSS Goals	x	Vocabulary use	x	Solve real-world issues	x	Discuss, interpret, explain
	x	Nonfiction use	x	Research	x	Use formal English
	x	Close reading	x	Build and present knowledge	x	Rigor
	x	Evidence-based claim		Text-based answers	x	Relevance

Rigor	Standards in the CCSS have been designed for college and career readiness. Research consistently identifies rote learning of math, practice with formulas, and memorization as strategies that fall short of deep understanding and formative knowledge. Manipulating, using, and applying mathematic concepts to the real-world require higher-level thinking. Explaining a concept with a model and applying a concept to the real-world both provide evidence of understanding. Mathematical thinking is needed to solve a problem and make sense of applications. Reasoning is involved in making a model or representation of a problem. Analysis and synthesis of nonfiction texts, many of which are technical, are rigorous. Communicating clearly and logically about complex and related functions is the final step in a rigorous process.
Relevance	The unit combines rigor with personal choices, even personal interests. It also has the potential to be fun. Real-world choices for the product boost relevance. They can also optimize motivation. Connecting slope to engineering, mechanics, construction, skiing, biking, hiking, safety, environmental issues, urban planning, architectural design, and

	access for the handicapped could turn the lights on regarding math. Texts contribute to a solution or a new idea. Sharing and modeling for peers, along with collaboration, make the project approach a relevant way to learn.
Reader and the task	Math students engaged in this lesson have an obvious purpose for reading, but will have to plan a research strategy that will help them succeed. They will literally have to break into the information environment, and open up areas where they will find their tools, their solutions, and their informational foundation. Keywords and discipline specific terms may need to be broadened or narrowed as pilot holes are dug in the information domain. Readers will need to make sense of technical language, mathematical illustrations, and complex ideas. Organization and planning will be needed to frame a model or representation. Readers will have to effectively navigating language, mathematical concepts, and effective communication.
Assessment	**Formative** Transparent thinking—Mind Map Checklist for process and expectations for the product Odell Research to Deepen Understanding graphic organizers for developing an inquiry question, for assessing sources, taking reflective notes, organizing and synthesizing Odell Evidence-based Claims Planning Guide- See www.odelleducation.com **Summative** Completed evidence-based claim Rubric for argument using evidence Rubric for multi-media project
Think-tank spotlight	• Develop abstract thinking and reasoning • Synthesize from multiple sources • Connect a concept to the real-world • Create a model, representation • Explaining by using concepts • Applying a concept • Gather, use, cite evidence • Evaluate, recognize misconceptions, validate • Plan, produce, create • Distinguishing relevance, usefulness • Think creatively • Begin to monitor and control thinking, plan • Begin to reason deductively • Prefer active learning and peer interaction • Infer and reason, drawing conclusions using thinking and not just experience • Solve problems • Move new learning into long-term memory when information connects with reality

Bloom's barometer	Remembering	Understanding	Applying	Analyzing	Evaluating	Creating
	X	X	X	X	X	X

From *Think Tank Library: Brain-Based Learning Plans for New Standards, Grades 6–12* by Mary Boyd Ratzer and Paige Jaeger. Santa Barbara, CA: Libraries Unlimited. Copyright © 2015.

Food, Water, Farming, and Shelter for a Changing Planet
Science and Math Infographic   Grade 7 or 8

WHAT'S THE BIG IDEA?

This interdisciplinary unit fuses scientific concepts, mathematical data, and an ELA evidence-based claim produced by a collaborative team of students. While discovering solutions to likely future problems for the planet, the learner manipulates, uses, and applies knowledge from mutually reinforcing disciplines of science and math. The thinking required to digest information and create an infographic progresses like this:

Transfer of the content is strengthened by the use of mathematical data to represent status quo problems such as:

- Food supply
- Water supply
- Hydrologic cycles
- Farming
- Shelter
- Erosion

In this lesson, students are required to support their conclusions with evidence about what the world needs to know now, to avoid a future problem (such as increased population and climate change). Transfer is further strengthened by using maps, data, and evidence to represent global supply and demand food, water, shelter, and farming success in the future, 25 years from now.

Engaging the collaborative learners in real-world problem solving provides a purpose for reading and analysis. Peer interaction encourages questioning, critical engagement, reflection, and metacognition. Thinking aloud, focus groups reviewing data at hand, and the ultimate development of an infographic that communicates an evidence-based claim refine the fuzzy thinking and surface notions of a middle school learner.

Teams will make evidence-based decisions regarding solutions to likely future problems. They will communicate the following in a mock Climate Change Forum:

- the status quo
- data-based predictions
- advocate for strategies using evidence

Local planners, farmers, government representatives, and higher education partners could be invited to witness the forum on climate change. Students are expected to create an infographic on climate change spotlighting a problem of their choice. Students can work in collaborative groups or individually based upon their interests.

Technology will enhance this lesson via research with databases, access to authoritative maps, graphical information, U.N. resources, and expert analysis. Technology also supports the development of an infographic to be shared with the community.

Sample close reading and data can be found in Climate Change 2014, A Report of the Intergovernmental Panel on Climate Change [http://.ipcc.ch].

Lesson:	Food, Water, Farming, and Shelter for a Changing Planet
Learning targets	Learners will synthesize science problems and data and represent these issues visually. Students will understand the possible impacts of climate change on humanity. Students will learn the cause and effect relationships of human choices can be supported with data. Learners will evaluate the authority of all information, and carefully sort fact from opinion.
Essential question	Why should we care about climate change?
Guiding questions	Has human behavior impacted our climate? How has human behavior impacted the Earth? Is there a cause and effect relationship between humanity and science? Can you identify major climate change issues? How have climate change issues manifested themselves? What should be done about climate change? How can we represent our data and conclusions in graphic format? What numbers or data make drastic comparisons to visualize?
Text	Science teachers are likely to be able to find a seed text for close reading and class discussion. From this close reading, students should be able to brainstorm real-world climate change effects. Possible seed text examples: • http://journalistsresource.org/studies/environment/climate-change/un-report-managing-climate-change/# • http://blogs.wsj.com/experts/2013/09/24/why-global-warming-is-different-and-harder-than-previous-environmental-problems/ • http://blogs.wsj.com/experts/2014/05/27/how-local-governments-lead-the-way-on-energy-policy/ Scientific periodicals at an appropriate Lexile; maps and graphs; and numerous publications from the United Nations are texts that can provide access to authoritative information, graphical analysis, verifiable predictions, and theories. http://www.ipcc.ch/ Consider other appropriate articles your collaborating science teacher chooses.
Power words	Comprehensive, erosion, biogeochemical, ethical, mitigating climate change, phenomena, prospective, scenario, vulnerability, and other power words that the class identifies and builds themselves. Allowing the students to build their own vocabulary of the discipline based upon the inquiry path they choose transfers ownership of the words and increases student accountability.

Vocabulary of library discipline	analyze, evaluate, synthesize, inquiry, critical thinking, problem solving, keywords, reliability, authority, representation, problem solving, evidence, data					
CCSS Goals	x	Vocabulary use	x	Solve real-world issues	x	Discuss, interpret, explain
	x	Nonfiction use	x	Research		Use formal English
	x	Close reading	x	Build and present knowledge	x	Rigor
	x	Evidence-based claim	x	Represent data	x	Relevance

Rigor	To understand climate change a student has to synthesize curriculum pieces. Students' logic will consider elements of cause and effect with change over time. This mental process is rigorous in addition to embracing rigorous reading. Representing data visually in an infographic requires a student understand and summarize key points convincingly.
Relevance	The daily news heightens students' awareness to climate change relevance. Wildfires, frequent tornados, Class 5 hurricanes, and changing weather patterns which have touched our communities and countries all contribute to a student's real-world relevance.
Reader and the task	After classroom close reading of a seed text, the teacher should ask text-dependent questions to activate thinking. Students should wonder and brainstorm questions for additional investigation, building an inquiry path. (Use the wonder question starters shown at the end of this lesson) In addition to the science content of this investigation, the following information literacy principles will be modeled and used: • Reads background information and brainstorms ideas • Considers opposing viewpoints • Recognizes diverse viewpoints and different insights • Crafts questions for investigation • Identifies quality information resources • Uses both facts and opinions appropriately • Paraphrases information appropriately and cites sources • Connects information to prior learning • Evaluates quality of information for credibility, accuracy, reliability, and timeliness • Analyzes and evaluates information to form evidence-based claim • Interprets information and ideas by defining, classifying, and inferring • Questions the differences among sources to resolve discrepancies • Forms opinions and judgments backed up by supporting evidence • Uses technology resources for investigation • Uses technology for knowledge product creation • Considers audience in knowledge product creation
Assessment	Formative Assessment: See graphic organizers in appendix to help guide students synthesis and understanding of data.

	Summative assessment: Work collaboratively with science and math teachers to create a rubric for the infographic. Include standards expectations for math, science, and information literacy. Students share their Infographics with each other. Display on whiteboard, print, or post on a class blog.
Think-tank spotlight	• Transition from concrete thinking to logical operations • Develop abstract thinking and reasoning • Store new information in short-term memory best when engaged • Store limited items in short-term memory at one time • Develop the ability to combine related items and classify them • Generalize • Think creatively • Begin to monitor and control thinking; plan • Begin to reason deductively • Begin to control impulses and coordinate thought and behavior • Prefer active learning and peer interaction • Infer and reason, drawing conclusions using thinking and not just experience • Transition to framing possibilities as well as facts and ideas without actual objects • Develop complex thinking and view of the world • Express personal thoughts and views and have intense interests • Focus on personal decision making, imagining outcomes of actions • Calculate mathematically • Solve problems • Test variables in a systematic manner • Question authority • Move new learning into long term memory when information connects with prior knowledge • Consider multiple perspectives of peers and others
Standards spotlight	**Common Core:** **Literacy in History, Science, Social Studies, and Technical Subject:** • Integrate quantitative or technical information expressed in words visually (e.g., in a flowchart, diagram, model, graph, or table). • Distinguish among facts, reasoned judgment based on research findings, and speculation in a text. • Cite specific textual evidence to support analysis of science and technical texts. • Determine the central ideas or conclusions of a text; provide an accurate summary of the text distinct from prior knowledge or opinions. • Introduce claim(s) about a topic or issue, acknowledge and distinguish the claim(s) from alternate or opposing claims, and organize the reasons and evidence logically. • Support claim(s) with logical reasoning and relevant, accurate data and evidence that demonstrate an understanding of the topic or text, using credible sources. • Introduce a topic clearly, previewing what is to follow; organize ideas, concepts, and information into broader categories as appropriate to achieve purpose; include formatting (e.g., headings) and graphics; develop the topic with relevant, well-chosen facts, definitions, concrete details, quotations, or other information and examples. • Conduct short research projects to answer a question (including a self-generated question), drawing on several sources and generating additional related, focused questions that allow for multiple avenues of exploration.

From *Think Tank Library: Brain-Based Learning Plans for New Standards, Grades 6–12* by Mary Boyd Ratzer and Paige Jaeger. Santa Barbara, CA: Libraries Unlimited. Copyright © 2015.

- Gather relevant information from multiple print and digital sources, using search terms effectively;
- Assess the credibility and accuracy of each source; and quote or paraphrase the data and conclusions of others while avoiding plagiarism and following a standard format for citation.
- Draw evidence from informational texts to support analysis reflection, and research.

[© Copyright 2010. National Governors Association Center for Best Practices and Council of Chief State School Officers. All rights reserved.]

Bloom's barometer	Remembering	Understanding	Applying	Analyzing	Evaluating	Creating
	x	x	x	x	x	x

QUESTION STEMS

Teaching a student to craft open-ended questions as well as concrete "fact" questions is often difficult. Based upon an elementary tool we created, this table below offers question starters to model the difference between asking surface fact versus deep meaning questions. Notice how the columns move from fact to meaning and deep meaning, left to right.

I wonder...	Define	How...
What	Describe	What if...
When	Explain	Should...
How	Identify	Why...
Who	Where	Could...
Where	Which	Would...
Which	Predict	Is there...

Digging Deeper for Meaning:
Topic: _____
Brainstorm Concrete Questions:

_____

_____

_____

_____

_____

_____

_____

Brainstorm meaning questions

Cause and effect; compare; contrast, use question prompt words: How, should, why, could, etc.

_____

_____

_____

_____

_____

_____

_____

_____

I wonder...	Define	How...
What	Describe	What if...
When	Explain	Should...
How	Identify	Why...
Who	Where	Could...
Where	Which	Would...
Which	Predict	Is there...

Evidence-Based Claim with Interpretation

Claim:
Evidence #1 (Data, quote, info or other piece of text supporting your claim):
Evidence #2:
Evidence #3:
Interpretation or Analysis

STEM: SCIENCE AND MATH LESSONS AND THINK-TANK STARTER KITS

Time to Launch Lessons for Your Brain Friendly Library!

Additional ideas are listed below to inspire you to build your own Inquiry-based learning endeavor with your teachers. Having read this book, you are likely equipped to develop deep student-centered learning endeavors from the ideas below.

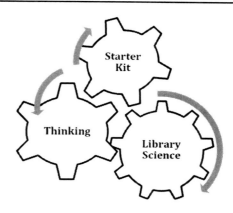

Text or Content	Inquiry Lessons in Science and Math
Hydro-fracking debate	EQ: Should hydraulic fracturing be approved for widespread use to solve the fossil fuel crisis?
	Debates are not for those who have surface knowledge informed by specious sources. Debates notch up the thinking to the expert level. A timely and controversial topic that lends itself to polarized views and inaccurate assumptions, hydro-fracking is debated by students in Earth Science, Chemistry, or Physics, since all of these contexts are relevant. Scientific thinking will guide students as they investigate all sides of the controversy, and require them to be objective.
	As students prepare for a debate on the topic, discerning fact from opinion is a primary concern. Evaluating the authority and perspective of sources involves higher level, critical thinking. This is a good content opportunity to teach Internet search skill scrutiny: • Google hits are treated with skepticism • Smart use of keywords can help bypass bias special interests • Exploring the sources of information for vested interest, expertise, and authority
	All this strengthens debate contentions and supporting evidence. Debaters filter for what is absolutely known. (See graphic organizer in appendix on fact versus opinion)
	Concept mapping is recommended as background knowledge builds into a map of complex big ideas. Students explore relationships among issues. Scientific data, expert testimony, accounts of alleged benefits and pitfalls, and proof of predictions and claims all align as pros and cons become explicit. Fuzzy, uninformed, general notions transform into cognitive bedrock.
	Taking a side means being ready to rebut the opposing points while substantiating key arguments. Speaking to the issue in a debate also requires genuine assimilation of broad knowledge which can be spontaneously accessed.
	Quality information resources address the process of hydro-fracking, its environmental impacts, or its safety. Estimates and data are needed regarding its production and potential production levels in the light of demand for natural gas. Further, its impact on landowners in depressed economies, its impact on property rights, and health considerations must be investigated and documented.
	Learners will read like detectives and write like reporters, adjusting their research questions as their knowledge grows.

	Science classes can participate in the debates, and provide an informed audience ready to critically listen and assess. Learning is student centered, engaging, and authentic.

Next Generation Science Standards:
Human Impacts on Earth Systems:
Engaging in Argument from Evidence:
Engaging in argument from evidence in grades 6–8 progresses to constructing a convincing argument that supports or refutes claims for either explanations or solutions about the natural and designed world(s).

• Construct an oral and written argument supported by empirical evidence and scientific reasoning to support or refute an explanation or a model for a phenomenon or a solution to a problem.
• Draw evidence from informational texts to support analysis, reflection, and research. |
| **My Math, My Health, My Plan** | **EQ: How can mathematical ratios represent my health now and inform the plan to improve health and fitness in my future?**

The context of this lesson is personal health and fitness that proceeds from self-assessment in specific areas of wellness. Planning and making informed decisions using math requires expert thinking. Adolescent learners certainly face a wake-up call from statistics about their health and fitness. Demographics are readily available and problems, such as obesity, calorie intake, exercise, sedentary behavior, hours spent gaming, or watching TV each day, dietary factors, BMI, consumption of soda, junk food habits, and even alcohol use or smoking emerge from the numbers.
• Students could be asked to brainstorm possible health-related concerns collaboratively.
• Students should build background knowledge by doing preliminary research in the percentages of fit teens versus teens who are not in shape.
• Students proceed from the big picture to analyze their own fitness using preselected tools provided by the American Heart Association, the Food and Drug Administration, Center for Disease Control, and other calculators that can determine a baseline number for the student in a particular area.
• Schools with fitness gyms can utilize gym equipment that reads out heart rates, METS, distance, or speed.
• In an information gathering effort, learners compile data to document their starting points in fitness, and then they compare their levels with optimal levels in a ratio.
• Students will chart their data and share their decisions and action plans.

An example might include a Body Mass Index (BMI) of 23 that puts a teen into the 95th percentile on the Center for Disease Control BMI chart. That would indicate that the teen is obese. The link below provides teens with information about BMI and a BMI percentile chart, along with a BMI calculator:
http://www.cdc.gov/healthyweight/assessing/bmi/childrens_bmi/about_childrens _bmi.html

For that teen's age and height, a BMI of 19 would be optimal. Using a ratio of real to optimal, the student uses quality information provided by the CDC to identify ways of eating healthy food and losing weight. That translates into a part of an action plan for that student, which is the product of this lesson. Indeed, that student can make a real-world decision about fitness using a ratio to make the decision. The action plan would include a timeline, strategic action, and a well thought-out goal documented with a target ratio.

Another example might be lowering calorie intake from 2300 a day, after using a calorie calculator, down to 1800 a day as a target. The ratio of real and optimal calorie consumption would drive a plan to modify diet. |

	Gym equipment that measures the METS of a learner on a treadmill at 4.5 gives that teen a baseline which reflects a low level of fitness and low cardio fitness. Working out to raise the METS to 11 during a workout gets that teen into a level of fitness that is much improved. Once again a real versus optimal ratio drives the action plan to change. Some changes might involve understanding of metabolic functions, the science of cardiovascular fitness, or how lifestyle choices affect fitness. Research to ensure understanding makes the learner responsible for his or her well-being. **Next Generation Science Standards:** **Mathematics Grades 6–8** • Understand the concept of a ratio and use ratio language to describe a ratio relationship between two quantities. • Recognize and represent proportional relationships between quantities. • Uses variables to represent numbers and write expressions when solving a real-world or mathematical problem
Epidemic!	**EQ: How is disease transmitted, and how can transmission be prevented?** Anyone who ever worked in a school was immersed in a germ pool of monumental pandemic proportions. This lesson provides the opportunity to replace a disease report with an experiment that is based on research. The disease report was aptly named because of its cut-and-paste, fact-packed nature—hardly meant for a healthy brain. • Learners build background knowledge on types of diseases, transmission, contamination, and prevention, and acquire a working vocabulary in the content area. This prepares them with an understanding of the big ideas of disease. • Class discussion included sharing articles about major epidemics, their spread worldwide, and the detective work done by the CDC and other agencies to track and pin down the agent causing the disease. Certainly the quest for a cure and prevention came into the big picture. Recent outbreaks of polio in the Middle East where vaccinations are prohibited, MERS virus which has no treatment and may come from contact with camels, SARS, bird flu, Norovirus on cruise ships, and good old-fashioned influenza are examples that might arise in discussion. • Students break into teams and brainstorm a way to study disease transmission and prevention in their middle school. They can research patterns of transmission and prevention in outbreaks in periodical literature and medical texts. • Students are prepared to create a mock discussion after their research and debate. Although no real symptoms or lethal germs are involved, the class plans an epidemic. The simple spread of an imaginary disease certainly raised the level of interest in the subject matter. Using a data-gathering model, they can initiate the epidemic with stickers placed on those who contract the disease from a contagious first case. The class carries out the task of observing and marking those contaminated by a pre-established path of transmission: students rubbing their eyes. After a day and a half the disease can be rampant, and some were afraid of catching it, even though it did not exist. Warnings and updates on the daily announcements kept the level of mock concern high. Analysis of the experimental data can help learners to draw conclusions and understand real-world occurrences of disease transmission. A little art work of the imaginary germ, a student body willing to cooperate, and curiosity finding its way to the school newspaper with a well-written scientific article about the epidemic are all possibilities.

	Next Generation Science Standards **Patterns** • Patterns can be used to identify cause-and-effect relationships. **Stability and Change** • Small changes in one part of a system might cause large changes in another part. Possible ELA novel to read along with this is *Code Orange* by Caroline Cooney.
Meet My Invasive Species	**EQ: How do invasive species adapt to compete in an ecosystem?** Students with an opportunity to observe invasive species draw conclusions about the adaptations that give these plants and animals a competitive edge in an ecosystem. Field work is combined with background building regarding a real-world invasive species problem. Databases and periodical accounts of these occurrences are combined with web-based resources that focus on addressing problems and solutions in an infected area. Students can create a graphic novel that conveys the science and exponential progress of invasive species which motivates and at the same time demonstrates understanding. By examining the root systems of invasive pants or the devastating success of invasive insects, students can narrate the science of life cycle, competition, advantageous adaptations, and damaging impact. A little Tim Burton darkness and a creepy root with boundless tendrils wiping out plants in its path could be a caricature of what is observed in the field and a great start for a compelling graphic novel about what happens when the delicate balance of living things is upset.
Carbon Atom Life Story **Biography of a Carbon Atom**	**EQ: What is the life story of a carbon atom?** A capstone project and certainly fun lesson at the end of a semester of Living Environment learning is the writing of a life story for a carbon atom. If a learner can use a storyboard or animation to tell a scientifically accurate tale of a carbon atom's life, that learner has to synthesize scientific learning and think analytically. Communicating the big picture in a simple sequence of slides requires deep and authentic understanding. "Well, it comes down to this." Since this may seem whimsical, students must grapple with the fact that carbon atoms do not begin and end their life cycle. They just keep cycling. One that starts in a fossil fuel deep underground is pulled up by an oil well, processed into a petroleum product, combusted in a gasoline engine, spewed out of exhaust system, escaped into the environment to hold heat in the atmosphere and contribute to global warming, and it does not end there. Of course every atom has its own story waiting to be told. Students research carbon atoms in order to build a biography of a carbon atom. Librarian and science teacher work cooperatively. This lesson was planned at a gathering of librarians and teachers in Eastern Suffolk BOCES, Bellport, New York, for grade 9.
Jig Saw the Periodic Table	**EQ: How did your chemical element change the world?** **EQ: How have our lives been impacted by the discovery and identification of this element?** An ELA novel whose rigor is appropriate for 11th-grade chemistry students is *The Disappearing Spoon* by Sam Kean. This engaging narrative nonfiction views the history of the world through the eyes of the periodic table. Students should be "hooked" with the preface to see that chemistry can be entertaining as well as relevant to their lives.

From *Think Tank Library: Brain-Based Learning Plans for New Standards, Grades 6–12* by Mary Boyd Ratzer and Paige Jaeger. Santa Barbara, CA: Libraries Unlimited. Copyright © 2015.

	Working collaboratively, ELA and Chemistry teachers can jigsaw this read (meaning break it up into chapters with each student, or collaborative group, taking an element or a couple elements). Each collaborative group meets as a book group to read and investigate the element and its impact on the world. Knowledge products do not have to be a written report, but could be a contribution to a "thinglink.com" of the Periodic Table. An alternative idea would be to use a periodic table and www.voicethread.com for students to voice their evidence-based claim on how their element changed history.
17 Molecules that changed the world	**EQ: How did your molecule shape the world?** **EQ: How was history impacted by the discovery of this molecule?** **EQ: Has your molecule's role changed over time?** Using the book *Napoleon's Buttons* by Penny Le Couteur and Jay Burreson, students can collaboratively read about their molecule and its impact on history. The entire book would be a rigorous read—a steady uphill climb. However, to read a chapter and be responsible for communicating the message is reasonable for a grade level that also studies chemistry and global history. This book looks at molecules and how products such as sugar, tin, or plastic impacted society in revolutionary ways. This brings relevance to a subject that is often separated from the application. Innovative knowledge sharing could be brainstormed by collaborative teachers to include débuts, debates over impacts, mock-chemists introducing their molecule to the world, and so forth.
Can statistics lie? Build a "Wall of Shame" Build a "Wall of Solid Claims"	**EQ: How can statistics be used to deceive, lie, or disguise the truth?** **EQ: Do advertisers, politicians, or other organizations use statistics to support their cause, candidate, or other message?** Spotlighting advertising, political advertising, or other deceptive statistics, teachers can ask students to scrutinize what they read, hear, or believe. Students can be sent on Inquiry Paths to investigate and scrutinize the way statistics are used. Math teachers and librarians can collaborate to discover sites, books, and data repositories for students to delve into. Students could be asked to "unpack" an advertisement and investigate whether that claim is solid or deceptive. Advertisers could be placed on one side of a wall or the other. Evidence-based claims should be used to solidly back up their views. Students should build a "Wall of Shame."

APPENDIX

In addition to the graphics found within each lesson, please find the following graphic organizers for your use.

Choosing a Path for Inquiry

Idea Path:	Idea Path:
Questions I have on this idea:	**Questions I have on this idea:**
Where I should look for this:	Where I should look for this:

From *Think Tank Library: Brain-Based Learning Plans for New Standards, Grades 6–12* by Mary Boyd Ratzer and Paige Jaeger. Santa Barbara, CA: Libraries Unlimited. Copyright © 2015.

Claim with Evidence

Claim or Conclusion:

Evidence, quotes, data, and other facts that support my claim: (indicate page numbers)

EVIDENCE-BASED CLAIM EVALUATION			
	Comments and Scoring		
Criteria	**Strong**	**Good Try**	**Next time try...**
Claim clearly stated			
Demonstrates your understanding			
Claim supported by text			
Sound thinking based upon evidence			
Uses direct quotations or text to support claim			
Explained thoroughly			
Includes vocabulary of the discipline			
Conclusion strongly summarized thinking			

Thinking about Evidence

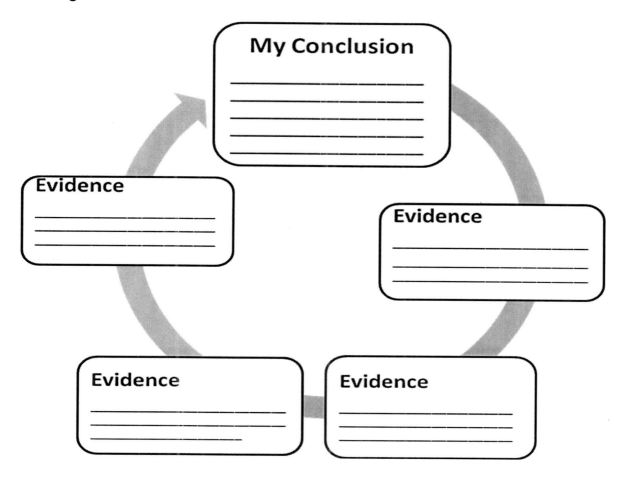

BIBLIOGRAPHY & RESOURCES

Abbott, John, and Terence Ryan. "Constructing Knowledge, Reconstructing Schooling." *Educational Leadership* November (1999): 66–69.

"Adolecence." In *Encyclopedia of Psychology*. Washington, D.C.: Oxford University Press, 2000.

"The Adolescent Brain: A Work in Progress—Pat Wolfe. Mind Matters, Inc." *Pat Wolfe Mind Matters Inc.* http://patwolfe.com/2011/09/the-adolescent-brain-a-work-in-progress/ (accessed May 14, 2014).

Barahal, Susan. "Thinking about Thinking." *Phi Delta Kappan* December (2008): 298–302.

Black, Susan. "Teachers Can Engage Disengaged Students." *Education Digest* 69, no. 7 (2004): 39–44.

Bransford, John, Ann L. Brown, and Rodney R. Cocking. *How People Learn Brain, Mind, Experience, and School.* Washington, D.C.: National Academy Press, 1999.

Bruer, John. "In Search of . . . Brain Based Education." *Phi Delta Kappan* May (1999): 80, 648–654, 656–657.

Bruer, John. "The Mind's Journey from Novice to Expert." *James S. McDonnell Foundation.* https://www.jsmf.org/about/j/minds_journey.htm (accessed January 16, 2014).

California State University, Northridge. "2 How Experts Differ from Novices." http://www.csun.edu/science/ref/reasoning/how-students-learn/2.html (accessed January 5, 2014).

Chall, Jeanne, and Vicki Jacobs. "The Classic Study on Poor Children's Fourth Grade Slump." *American Educator* Spring (2003). http://www.aft.org/newspubs/periodicals/ae/spring2003/hirschsbclassic.cfm (accessed February 24, 2004).

"Childhood Years Ages Six through Twelve." *NC State University.* http://www.ces.ncsu.edu/depts/fcs/pdfs/fcs465. pdf (accessed February 11, 2014).

Choudhury, Suparna, Sarah-Jayne Blakemore, and Tony Charman. "Social Cognitive Development during Adolescence." *Social Cognitive and Affective Neuroscience* 1, no. 3 (2006): 165–174. http://www.ncbi.nlm.nih.gov/pmc/articles/PMC2555426/ (accessed January 13, 2014).

Chugani, Harry. "A Critical period of Brain Development: Studies of Cerebral Glucose Utilization with PET." *Preventive Medicine* 7 (1998): 184–188.

Ciardiello, A. Vincent. *Puzzle Them First!: Motivating Adolescent Readers with Question-Finding.* Newark, Del.: International Reading Association, 2007.

"Cognitive Development in Middle Childhood." *KU Department of Psychology.* http://psych.ku.edu/dennisk/CP333/Cognitive%20Middle.pdf (accessed February 4, 2014).

Cognitive Development, University of Rochester Medical Center. http://www.urmc.rochester.edu/Encyclopedia/Content.aspx?ContentTypeID=90&ContentID=P01594 (accessed February 20, 2014).

"College, Career, and Civic Life (C3) Framework for Social Studies State Standards." *National Council for the Social Studies.* http://www.socialstudies.org/c3 (accessed May 14, 2014).

Columbia University Teaching Center. "Transformational Teaching." Columbia.edu. http://www.columbia.edu/cu/tat/pdfs/Transformational%20Teaching.pdf (accessed May 9, 2014).

"The Common Core State Standards Develop Thinking." Center for Urban Education. http://teacher.depaul.edu/Documents/Common_Core_Toolkit.pdf (accessed March 21, 2014).

"Designing Inquiry Based Science Units." *A Community Approach for a Sustainable Growth of Science Education in Europe. Seed Cities for Science.* http://www.fondationlamap.org/sites/default/files/upload/media/Guide _Designing%20and%20implementing%20IBSE_final_light.pdf (accessed February 17, 2014).

Donovan, Suzanne, and John Bransford. *How Students Learn History, Mathematics, and Science in the Classroom.* Washington, D.C.: National Academies Press, 2005.

Duschl, Richard A., Heidi A. Schweingruber, and Andrew W. Shouse. *Taking Science to School: Learning and Teaching Science in Grades K-8.* Washington, D.C.: National Academies Press, 2007.

"Educational Psychology Interactive: Cognitive Development." Piaget's Theory of Cognitive Development. http://www.edpsycinteractive.org/topics/cognition/piaget.html (accessed February 17, 2014).

"English Language Arts Standards." *Home.* http://www.corestandards.org/ELA-Literacy/ (accessed May 14, 2014).

"Experts vs. Novices: What Students Struggle with Most in STEM Disciplines." *Arizona State University.* http://modeling.asu.edu/Projects-Resources/HarperK-ExpertVsNovice.pdf (accessed March 18, 2014).

Harada, Violet. "Empowered Learning: Fostering Thinking Across the Curriculum." *University of Hawaii.* http://www2.hawaii.edu/~vharada/Empowered.pdf (accessed June 9, 2009).

Harvard Univerity. "ALPS: The Thinking Classroom: Ways of Thinking." http://learnweb.harvard.edu/alps/thinking/ways.cfm (accessed March 29, 2013). Harvard University. "Artful Thinking." Project Zero. http://www.pz.gse.harvard.edu/artful_thinking.php (accessed May 15, 2014).

Harvard University. "Visible Thinking." http://www.visiblethinkingpz.org (accessed May 2, 2011).

Harvey, Stephanie, and Anne Goudvis. *Strategies that Work: Teaching Comprehension to Enhance Understanding.* York, Me.: Stenhouse Publishers, 2000.

Hess, Karin. "Applying Webb's Depth of Knowledge (DOK) Levels in Social Studies." *NCIEA.* http://www.nciea.org/publications/DOKsocialstudies_KH08.pdf (accessed July 1, 2012).

Hess, Karin. "Applying Webb's Depth of Knowledge (DOK) Levels in Science." *NCIEA.* http://www.nciea.org/publications/DOKscience_KH11.pdf (accessed July 1, 2012).

Hess, Karin. "Applying Webb's Depth of Knowledge (DOK) Levels in Reading." *bllblogs.* http://bllblogs.typepad.com/files/dokreading_kh08.pdf (accessed July 1, 2012).

Hess, Karin. "Applying Webb's Depth of Knowledge (DOK) Levels in Writing." *NCIEA.* http://www.nciea.org/publications/DOKwriting_KH08.pdf (accessed July 1, 2012).

Hess, Karin. "Hess Cognitive Rigor Matrix & Curricular Examples." *PEDSAS,* http://static.pdesas.org/content/documents/M1-Slide_22_DOK_Hess_Cognitive_Rigor.pdf (accessed July 1, 2012).

Hester, Joseph. *Teaching for Thinking.* Durham, North Carolina: Carolina Academic Press, 1994.

Hirsch, E. D. "Seeking Breadth and Depth in the Curriculum." *Educational Leadership* October (2001): 22–25.

Hirsch, E. D. "Reading Comprehension Requires Knowledge - of Words and the World." *American Educator* Spring (2003): 10–29.

Hoberman, Mary Ann, and Michael Emberley. *You Read to Me, I'll Read to You: Very Short Stories to Read Together.* Boston: Little, Brown, 2001.

"Inquiry in Mathematics Supporting Kindergarten." *Saskatchewan Online Curriculum.* http://curriculum.nesd.ca/Supporting_Docs/Math_K/Inquiry%20in%20Mathematics.pdf (accessed May 13, 2011).

Intel. "Designing Effective Projects: Thinking Skills Frameworks Marzano's New Taxanomy." *Marzano's New Taxanomy.* http://download.intel.com/education/Common/in/Resources/DEP/skills/Marzano.pdf (accessed April 12, 2013).

Jaeger, Paige. "Repackaging Research." *School Library Monthly* September/October (TBP, 2014).

Jaeger, Paige. "Think, Jane, Think. See Jane Think. Go, Jane. Metacognition and Learning in the Library." *Library Media Connection* 26, no. 3 (2007): 18–21.

Johnson, Ben. *Teaching Students to Dig Deeper: The Common Core in Action.* Larchmont: Eye on Education, 2013.

Johnson, Doug. "Right Brain Skills and the Media Center." *American Library Association.* http://www.ala.org/aasl/aaslpubsandjournals/knowledgequest/kqwebarchives/v35/354/354johnson (accessed July 16, 2008).

"The Journey from Novice to Expert." *When Knowing Matters.* http://www.whenknowingmatters.com/the-journey -from-novice-to-expert/ (accessed January 16, 2014).

King, F. J., Ludwika Goodson, and Faranak Rohani. "Higher Order Thinking Skills." *Center for Advancement of Learning and Assessment.* http://www.cala.fsu.edu/files/higher_order_thinking_skills.pdf (accessed October 18, 2012).

Krynock, Karoline, and Louise Robb. "Problem Solved: How to Coach Cognition." *Educational Leadership* November (1999): 29–32.

Kuhlthau, Carol Collier, Ann K. Caspari, and Leslie K. Maniotes. *Guided Inquiry Learning in the 21st Century.* Westport, Conn.: Libraries Unlimited, 2007.

Lackaff, Julie, and Cynthia Hoisington. "Scientific Thinking." *NCS Pearson.* http://images.pearsonclinical.com/images/Assets/WSS_5/Research_Summary_Scientific_Thinking_FNL.pdf (accessed November 25, 2013).

Levine, Mel. "The Essential Cognitive Backpack." *Educational Leadership* 64, no. 7 (2007): 16–22.

Marzano Center. "Common Core on a Mission—Marzano Center." http://www.marzanocenter.com/blog/article/common-core-on-a-mission/ (accessed February 27, 2014).

"Mathematics Standards." *Home.* http://www.corestandards.org/Math/ (accessed May 12, 2014).

"Metacognition." http://www.etc.edu.cn/eet/Articles/metacognition/start.htm (accessed January 3, 2014).

Missouri department of Elementary and Secondary Education. "Research and Proven Practices." *MSTA.* http://www.msta.org/wp-content/uploads/2013/08/eq-ees-resources.pdf (accessed February 11, 2014).

The National Academy of Sciences. How People Learn. Brain, Mind, Experience, and School: Expanded Edition. http://www.nap.edu/openbook.php?record_id=9853&page=31 (accessed January 3, 2014).

National Governors Association Center for Best Practices and Council of Chief State School Officers. "Common Core State Standards Initiative." Home. http:www.corestandards.org (accessed June 14, 2011).

NCTE. "NCTE Framework for 21st Century Curriculum and Assessment." *NCTE Comprehensive News.* http://www.ncte.org/governance/21stcenturyframework (accessed February 21, 2012).

NEA. "12 Principles for Brain-Based Learning." *National Education Association.* http://edweb.sdsu.edu/people/cmathison/armaitiisland/files/BBLrngPrin.pdf (accessed November 20, 2013).

NEA. "Brain Development in Young Adolescents." *National Education Association.* http://www.nea.org/tools/16653.htm (accessed January 13, 2014).

"The Next Generation Science Standards | Next Generation Science Standards." The Next Generation Science Standards | Next Generation Science Standards. http://www.nextgenscience.org/next-generation-science-standards (accessed May 13, 2014).

Newmann, Fred, and Gary Wehlage. "Five Standards of Authentic Instruction." *Educational Leadership* April (1993): 8–12.

Novak, Katie. *UDL Now! A Teacher's Monday-Morning Guide to Implementing Common Core Standards Using Universal Design for Learning.* Wakefield, Massachusetts: CAST Publishing Company, 2014.

"The Novice Brain." The eLearning Coach. http://theelearningcoach.com/learning/the-novice-brain/ (accessed December 21, 2013).

Odell Education. "Unit 2: Making Evidence-Based Claims—Odell Education." Odell Education RSS2. http://odelleducation.com/making-ebc-lesson (accessed October 23, 2013).

Partnerships for Assessment of Readiness for College and Careers. "ARCC Model Content Frameworks English Language Arts/Literacy." *Parcconline.* http://www.parcconline.org/sites/parcc/files/PARCCMCFELALiteracy August2012_FINAL.pdf (accessed February 18, 2013).

Pink, Daniel. *A Whole New Mind.* New York: Riverhead Books, 2005.

Railsback, Jennifer. "Project=Based Instruction: Creating Excitement for Learning." *Northwest Regional Laboratory.* http://educationnorthwest.org/webfm_send/460 (accessed August 5, 2012).

Ritchhart, Ron, and David Perkins. "Making Thinking Visible." *Educational Leadership* 65, no. 5 (2008): 57–61. http://www.visiblethinkingpz.org/VisibleThinking_html_files/06_AdditionalResources/makingthinkingvisibleEL.pdf (accessed January 19, 2009).

Savoie, Joan, and Andrew Hughes. "Problem-Based Learning as Classroom Solution." *Educational Leadership* November (1994): 54–57.

Small, Gary W., and Gigi Vorgan. *iBrain: Surviving the Technological Alteration of the Modern Mind.* New York: Collins Living, 2008.

Southwest Educational Development Laboratory. "SEDL - SCIMAST Classroom Compass." *How Can Research on the Brain Inform Education.* http://www.sedl.org/scimath/compass/v03n02/brain.html (accessed March 11, 2014).

Tate, Marcia L. *Worksheets Don't Grow Dendrites: 20 Instructional Strategies that Engage the Brain.* Thousand Oaks, Calif.: Corwin Press, 2003.

Tishman, Shari. "The Object of their Attention." *Educational Leadership* 65, no. 5 (2008): 44–46. http://www.ascd.org/publications/educational-leadership/feb08/vol65/num05/The-Object-of-Their-Attention.aspx (accessed January 17, 2009).

Tishman, Shari, and Patricia Palmer. "Visible Thinking." *Leadership Compass.* http://www.visiblethinkingpz.org/ VisibleThinking_html_files/06_AdditionalResources/VT_LeadershipCompass.pdf (accessed April 28, 2013).

Twenge, Jean M. *Generation Me: Why Today's Young Americans Are More Confident, Assertive, Entitled—and More Miserable Than Ever Before.* New York: Free Press, 2006.

Vanderbilt University. "How People Learn, The Nature of Expertise." *CFT RSS.* http://cft.vanderbilt.edu/guides sub-pages/how-people-learn/ (accessed December 21, 2013).

"Virtual Information Inquiry: Pathways to Knowledge" *Virtual Information Inquiry: Student Information Scientists and Instructional Specialists in the Learning Laboratory.* http://virtualinquiry.com/ (accessed December 21, 2013).

Washington State Department of Early Learning. "Washington State Early Learning and Development Guidelines." *Department of Early Learning Page.* http://www.del.wa.gov/development/guidelines/ (accessed February 9, 2014).

Willingham, Daniel. "Inflexible Knowledge: The First Step to Expertise." *American Educator* Winter (2002): 31–49.

Willingham, Daniel. "Why Students Think They Understand—When They Don't." *American Educator* Winter (2004). http://www.aft.org/newspubs/periodicals/ae/winter0304/willingham.cfm (accessed February 24, 2004).

Wolfe, Patricia. *Brain Matters: Translating Research into Classroom Practice*, 2nd Edition. Alexandria, Virginia: ASCD, 2010.

Worth, Karen. "Science in Early Childhood Classrooms: Content and Process." *SEED Papers* Fall (2010): 1–11. http://ecrp.uiuc.edu/beyond/seed/worth.html (accessed April 12, 2014).

Wunderlich, Khaki, Annette Bell, and Lisa Ford. "Improving Learning Through Understanding of Brain Science Research." *Learning Abstracts* 8, no. 1 (2005): 41–43.

INDEX

ABOUT THE AUTHORS

MARY BOYD RATZER is a professional development consultant who fosters inquiry-based learning and real-world strategies for the Common Core. Formerly, she served as a teacher and school librarian at the Shenendehowa Central Schools in New York, and taught curriculum as an adjunct faculty at UAlbany's Graduate School of Information Studies. Her published works include Libraries Unlimited's *Rx for the Common Core: Toolkit for Implementing Inquiry Learning* and the American Association of School Librarians' (AASL) *Knowledge Quest on the C3 Frameworks for Social Studies State Standards.* Ratzer holds a master's degree in library science and a master's degree in the arts.

PAIGE JAEGER delivers professional development at the local, state, and national levels and is currently serving on the AASL Task Force for the Common Core. Previously, she was a library administrator serving 84 school libraries in New York. Her published works include Libraries Unlimited's *Rx for the Common Core: Toolkit for Implementing Inquiry Learning* and articles in *School Library Journal, School Library Monthly, Library Media Connection,* and AASL's *Knowledge Quest on the C3 Frameworks for Social Studies State Standards.* She holds a certificate of advanced study and a master's degree in library science.

Mary and Paige often travel together delivering full-day and multi-day professional development for educators.

CPSIA information can be obtained at www.ICGtesting.com
Printed in the USA
BVOW04s0346060516

446724BV00009B/112/P